Practical
Pre-School Books

34065

Outdoor Pl

D0198777

Play in the EYFS

Contents

Published by Practical Pre-School Books , A Division of MA Education
St Jude's Church, Dulwich Road, Herne Hill, London, SE24 0PB Tel 020 7738 5454
© Practical Pre-School Books, A Division of MA Education 2009
www.practicalpreschoolbooks.com

Play in the EYFS: Outdoor Play ISBN: 978-1-90457-598-6

Outdoor Play

Contents continued

Not all children attend well-equipped nurseries with exciting and challenging outdoor areas. Some go to village halls or community centres with little or no access to an outside area, some go to nurseries attached to schools and some children play in someone's front room! But all early years settings should be providing outside play opportunities regardless of their facilities.

All groups of children are different but in every group there will be some children who learn best when they are outside. To make it easier for these children to learn, you need an environment that is safe, inviting, stimulating and challenging. No matter how small the space, it can be made interesting, even if the equipment has to be set up and stored away each day. Those settings that have no outdoor space available to them could think about investigating the local park, woodland area and immediate surrounding area.

Ideally, the children should be able to move from the indoor to the outdoor areas with minimum fuss, but this is not always possible. Some settings have areas available to them but they are not attached to their indoor space. Careful planning is the answer. It may be that groups of children go to the area at one time. This is not ideal and care must be taken that all of the children are given equal access; this means those that want to go outside can rather than 'It's your turn now so you must go'.

In many settings children go outside only when the weather is warm and sunny. This is often not the children's choice but the adults! Children don't notice the weather and will choose to go outside even when it is cold and rainy. If they are equipped with wellies and macs they should be outside. How else will they have the experience of just being in the rain? Smelling it? Seeing puddles form and jumping in them? Watching the stream of water coming from the downpipe? Wondering where all the water goes?

Outdoor play is as important as indoor play. Space, fresh air, freedom and time are essential for children's emotional, social and personal well-being.

Outdoor play is vital because:

- It enables children to become independent learners. Children should enjoy learning and you can help them to develop that all-important disposition to learn by providing them with an environment which they can explore, modify and use themselves. If they need to keep asking you for equipment or resources you are taking away their independence.

  You can invite the children to make choices, follow their own interests and get involved with what they are doing. For some children the outdoors is where they are most comfortable.

- It encourages social and moral development. Outdoor play presents opportunities for exploring and using large equipment. This involves children in taking turns, sharing, cooperating, negotiating and talking to each other - all essential skills when interacting with other people in a positive way. They will establish relationships and begin to understand that others have feelings and emotions, for example seeing friends become upset when hurt, and being able to empathise.

- It encourages children to grow in confidence and self-esteem.
  Some children appear more comfortable with themselves and others when they are outside. They play with confidence in the knowledge that they can be noisier and more boisterous and they do not feel as restricted as they may do indoors.

  Confidence and self-esteem are crucial for children's well-being and ability to learn. Those children who are given opportunities to achieve success, whether it is through being able to be good at climbing or being leader in an imaginative game, are the most likely to enjoy satisfaction and a feeling of well-being. They will want more.

- It promotes and enables physical activity. Joining in physical activity can have huge benefits for

young children. It can help them to cope with success and failure in a supported environment and to develop a sense of fair play.

It makes a unique contribution to the development of the whole child and research evidence suggests there is a link between physical activity and academic achievement, as well as an improvement in children's behaviour and the development of social interaction (Using Physical Activity and Sport DfES 2000).

Giving children the choice to be outside is a powerful tool. Conflicts can be resolved more easily and imaginative, well planned, challenging areas for children with diagnosed behavioural problems can often result in calmer, more interested children.

We all know young children need space, as movement is central to their development and learning. Their motor development is at a crucial stage and they need to be given opportunities to strengthen their large muscles to improve the control of their smaller ones. (To write with control they will need to develop their arm and shoulder muscles as well as their hand and finger muscles.)

- It allows children to take risks.
  Children's safety is of paramount importance and you need to be mindful when planning the outside area but too many restrictions can reduce choice and make children dependent on adults. Children will take risks in their play that they are comfortable with because they set their own agenda.

- It allows time to consolidate skills learned.
  Children need time to repeat, mimic, and try once more the skills they have been learning. Sometimes this may be through giving them the time alone. At other times it may be through providing for the same skills with a wider range of activities and experiences that may be bigger, noisier, messier than those offered indoors.

Good practice

Whatever facilities you have available, good practice in outdoor play means that the children are in the most effective teaching and learning situation. They will be given challenges that are both exciting and stimulating so that they want to find out more. The adults will be supporting and intervening at appropriate times because they have observed the children and know at what stage to intervene in order to carry them forward. (Sometimes the children are best left to do this for themselves.)

Good practice means:

- that, if possible, the children can go outside whenever they need to;
- planning what the children will experience so that their learning is seamless and interlinked and enables them to join up their thinking;
- the area is so organised that the children understand the systems, for example where to get equipment if they want it, what to do if they need help;
- that the children themselves can change and modify the area to suit their methods of play at that time;
- having an area that is versatile so that the children can look forward every day to something that is stimulating for them. Sometimes if children are working on a project they do not want to put it away at the end of the day or session. Being versatile means being able to accommodate their needs and leaving it so the children can go back to refine it until it has run its course;
- having committed staff and helpers who understand the value of children playing outside.

Wychbold First School and Nursery (16 children, mornings only, age three plus) is part of a school building with a large outdoor area, part grass, part tarmac with an undercover area.

- The resources and equipment for the week are planned according to the interests of the children shown in the previous week.
- Each morning the equipment is set out by the nursery teacher and the school caretaker.
- The children spend the first part of the morning inside, talking and actively engaged in being part of the whole group - listening, discussing, contributing and finding out about each other.
- From 9.20am the door is open to the outside area and children can come and go as they please. One adult is always outside and one inside. The adults are skilled at knowing when to intervene and when to stand back. Sometimes another item of equipment may be brought out because of the way the play is progressing. Children are encouraged to experiment for themselves, fetch and carry for themselves and to be responsible for the resources and equipment.
- Occasionally, the group is brought together to watch something or look at a model built by one or more or to tell everyone what they have found.
- The children move freely from inside to outside and will often mimic the type of activities inside and out, for example: Sam was keen to explore the logs outside. He spent a long time transporting them with Callum to the large tractor tyres. When this task was completed to their satisfaction, Callum and Sam sat proudly on the top of the tyres. Sam said 'I've built a house'. Callum said 'I've made a fire for the house' and began to warm his hands. Later Sam chose to paint at the indoor easel. The newspaper used to protect the easel had a photograph of a man working with trees and sawing enormous logs. Sam said 'Look! Those are just like the logs we built the house with outside. I'm going to paint my picture of the logs!'

Inside Amy enjoyed the marble rolling activity. She was keen to sprinkle the paint from her spoon to create a pattern on her paper. Outside Amy chose to explore the sandy mud. Using the same sprinkling action she created sandy patterns on the paving slabs outside.

- There is a plenary session in the form of fruit and drinks mid morning when children can share what they have been doing if they want to.
- The adults are sensitive to those children who want to work on things started on another day that they need time to finish.

Mayfield House Kindergarten is in an old, large rambling house with a well-established garden and orchard area. The kindergarten has babies through to four-year-olds and has a strong emphasis on encouraging exploration and enjoyment of nature, maintaining good social values and sharing with the children the joy of discovery and achievement.

All through the year outside there is:

- Sand
- Large-scale blocks
- Natural building materials
- Digging/gardening

- Bikes/trucks
- Balls
- Water/pipes/buckets
- The children are free to choose to go outside and outdoor clothing is supplied.

Here are some of the activities the children had fun with in the autumn:

- Colours - natural materials, rainbows, colour story walk, swatch matching, bark rubbing, pattern making.
- Trees – leaves, seeds, 'Come little leaves' song and dance.
- Squirrel hunts and treasure hiding, maps.
- Building nesting boxes, bird feeding tables, hedgehog houses.
- Leaf sweeping and sorting, compost making, den making, hiding the mouse in a pile, trail making, making sounds.
- Wind – kite making, leaf threading, mobiles, chimes, seed catching.
- Gardening – harvest - pumpkins/squashes, digging soil for spring planting, planting bulbs and garlic, clearing and composting.

- Apples – picking, sorting, counting, transporting, storing, eating, apple bobbing, printing.
- Pumpkin carving – Jack o' lantern song, 'Five little pumpkins'.
- Role play - farmers' market, animal food store.
- Treasure boxes
- Mini gardens

Children learn best through making sense of the world. This means you need to provide every opportunity for the children in your care to reenact the world around them so they can see their place, where they fit in and how it all fits together. For them to have quality learning through play experiences you have to work hard!

All of the adults in your setting need to be involved in the planning that will go on beforehand. They will need to think about the resources required and where the equipment is to be set up.

The indoor experiences sometimes need to be linked with the outdoor experiences, so that skills tried indoors can be encountered outside and reinforced or consolidated. Your outdoor play area should fit the needs of your particular group of children – both as a whole group and as individuals. If the area is very small, all the more reason to treat it as an extension to the indoor area and use it in the same way that the role-play, construction or creative areas are used. If the area is very large, children can feel intimidated and lost. Adults almost become supervisors rather than actively engaging with the children.

Different experiences

The original design of the outdoor space is obviously important and sometimes it is difficult to make sure that the children are offered different experiences. Perhaps a tarmac square is the only outside provision you have and the children love riding around it on their bikes – it is ideal for it! But when do the children have the chance to dig, find buried treasure or look for insects? It is important that a broad range of activities and experiences are available to them and this should be planned so that for some part of the year the bikes are put away and, for example, plant tubs and boxes for digging are put in the area instead.

All areas of learning and development can be promoted outdoors and careful consideration should be made when planning the resources and activities that will lead to exploration for children. Remember to make use of the space. More space means freedom for children to be active in their learning. A language game could be to run to the corner, go under the climbing apparatus, over the crate, and so on. A numeracy game could be how quickly they can find the six objects you have hidden – use a large timer to check.

In an ideal world the children are able to go in and out of the outdoor area as they please. Perhaps they indicate in some way that they are outdoors – putting their names on a Velcro chart, for instance. There could be times when all the children want to be outside. Is there enough room for this? If not, the system would have to indicate that no more can go outside just yet.

Children need to find out about the world around them, make sense of their discoveries and discover their own culture. They need a way to do this for themselves and you, as a practitioner, need to help them find their way and accommodate them.

Links with indoor activities

There is clearly a link between the indoor and outdoor areas. Children do not just switch off one mode of learning inside and switch on another for outside. They learn in a seamless way and you cannot divorce the inside from the outside. If a child was engrossed with the train set inside they will more often or not play at trains outside whether it is racing around pretending to be a train or building a track in the sand or mud. So planning needs to be linked.

The practice guidance document for the early years (in England) is divided into six areas of learning and development. We know that children do not learn in this neat way, but for the purposes of planning it is easier to look at these areas with planning for the outdoors in mind. In this way you can make sure that all children are offered the fullest range of opportunities possible, within their needs and capabilities.

Observation and assessment

Quotes from 'The Early Years Foundation Stage: Effective practice: the Learning Environment'

Adults should tune into children's interests and interact with them to support and extend their learning and development, jointly engaging in problem solving and sustained shared thinking.

Adults should respond to observed interests and plan new materials and experiences within the environment that reflect these.

For adults to be able to 'tune in' to children's interests and 'respond', a system of observing, assessing, planning and reviewing is of paramount importance. The system needs to be constant and uncompromising and

- be simple to follow,
- allow everyone connected to the child to take part,
- enable very clear succinct notes about the child's learning to take place and have a clear structure and reasoning behind the next steps planned.

Adults will need to be expert at observing what is happening within the play and be able to write quick notes so that it is meaningful later in the day when the notes are fed back.

This process is essential so that resources, ideas and themes can be planned on a day to day basis so that the children are constantly stimulated and encouraged to learn.

Adults need to feel that their observations and assessments are guiding the children's learning. Often adults feel swamped by the observation and assessment process.

Example of practice

Practitioners wear 'money belt' type bags around the waist with pens, 'post-it' pads, Dictaphones and a 'What to look for' card attached to a key-ring on a chain. (See an example of what to look for using the Observation template for weekly outdoor play at the end of this section).

Carrying items in this way means it is quick to jot notes on the pad – they are always available. It is so easy to put a notepad down on a shelf or table and lose it! The 'What to look for' card lists the specific objectives - what you are really trying to observe, and give confidence to those adults who are not too sure about what to write down. Sometimes too much general information is collected as 'observation'. Less is more in these situations

The 'post-it' jottings are collected every day and sorted, so that the significant ones are kept, but others thrown away. The significant ones could be those that show a child:

- has understood a concept,
- is able to do something new,
- has used different and more complex vocabulary (captured by a Dictaphone maybe?),
- has shown a step forward in social interaction, or a direct observation of one of the key points from the 'What to look for' card.

The results of the discussions following the observations are linked directly to the planning for the resources, experiences and activities that will be offered for the next few days and, as the process is so fluid, the children's interests are followed and incorporated.

The weekly planning sheet also needs to be flexible with plenty of space for ideas and activities to be added as the week progresses. You cannot know on Monday what the children will want to explore on Friday! (See the example of planning sheet at the end of this section). On the plan there is space for staff to put their initials beside the times or days that they will be outside.

There are no separate indoor or outdoor planning sheets. Activities and experiences should be planned in such a way that they can be both indoor and outdoor. Again, this has to be flexible to allow for the children's own interests, although generally most children could choose to go outside for a large part of their time.

Planning should be simple and straightforward and not a cottage industry in itself. If adults and children are involved in the process it becomes a natural part of daily life.

In headings below are suggestions for observations of outdoor play across the six areas of learning and development.

Personal, Social and Emotional Development

- Do the children help to plan the outdoor area and get the resources for the day/week?
- Do you give them the chance to decide and explain why they would like certain items of equipment in the area that week?
- Do you plan for cooperative play? (for example, helping each other to put up the tent)
- Turn taking is always fraught. Do you plan for games and activities that encourage turn taking?
- Can the children choose their own resources? Are they in boxes at a level the children can manage themselves? Are they always in the same place so that all children will become confident in trying something new?
- Can the children manage the transition from inside to outside independently, for example is there

somewhere for them to store their shoes, put on wellies and macs, and is there a way that shows who is outside?
- Have you planned how to bring the children together quickly if necessary? Is there a way a child can attract attention, such as a bell under a plant pot?

These questions all encourage the children to become independent and confident and should be included in your planning as part of Personal, Social and Emotional Development.

Communication, Language and Literacy

Children need positive experiences of early communication so that they are likely to be confident and go on to enjoy conversation, reading and writing. Planning for language and literacy experiences outdoors does not mean putting pencils and paper on a table outside, neither does it mean taking a book outside but a quality play activity could include both of these.

Books and stories allow children to explore the wider world whilst dealing with some of their fears and passions. Drama and poetry allow children to realise there is more than one way of doing things.

- If listening and speaking skills need improving, can you plan for this to be a focus when outdoors? Is there a quiet corner that invites children to listen and talk to each other? Can they listen to tapes and stories outside?
- Do you plan for children to talk and interact with each other? Is there an imaginary/role-play area set up for them? Do you have a variety of prop boxes to support their play? (see pages 21-23)
- Sometimes children communicate by just being with each other – not necessarily speaking. This can be valuable for children who need confidence.

- Do you encourage them to find a shady nook and a blanket and browse through the story books?
- Some stories are wonderful for acting out and children will often put their own interpretations to stories. They will change the endings or even begin to introduce new characters – the beginning of writing stories for themselves.
- Is there an area where the children can make marks? Not just blackboards/whiteboards but somewhere where they can use a stick to write in mud or sand?
- Do you plan for activities where the children can go and get a clipboard and writing tool because they need to record something?
- Are there large sheets of paper fixed to a wall or fence or on the ground where the children can practise drawing large pictures?
- Do they see print around their play area that means something to them? Perhaps it's a menu of what they can buy at the café or a price list for petrol at the garage. If it is meaningless to them they will not bother to look.
- There are many fun games that involve hunting for buried treasure. These may be objects, letters or words but all of these types of games encourage children to be focused.

Problem Solving, Reasoning and Numeracy

Many people find this the hardest area to plan for when playing outside. However, do not get too constrained by the idea that maths is counting. Outside is about having space and many children need to come to terms just with that idea. Then, when you look at the space available to your children, what do you see? Is there room for that huge box you brought in for them to play with? The children can be part of the decision-making process. Let them decide where the best place is. Maybe your area is large enough for there to be segregated areas for different types of play. How many areas? Again, the children can be part of the process.

- Plan for the children to be part of the process when setting up the play area sometimes.
- Introduce activities that will include mathematical vocabulary. Sometimes use stories that will help.
- When children play they will often be counting or matching one to one. Include lots of play situations that will encourage this, for example the three bears story, making mud pies, giving each animal on the farm some food. Plan for as many of these kinds of experiences as possible so that they make sense to the children. You are not asking them to count in a vacuum.
- Physical play or catching games, with an adult, can include lots of calculations.
- Plan for the kinds of activities that mean the children have to collect three of one and three of another – always popular!
- Use your wheeled vehicles so they enhance the maths in your group. Put number plates on them for a week and set up a garage in your role play. Talk about and help children to recognise patte
- Delivering games are popular – where the postman or postwoman takes two letters to teddy by the toy shed and four letters to the clown in the corner. Plan for these activities so that by the end of the week/two weeks all of the children have had the chance to be the postman or postwoman.
- The beauty of outdoor play is that everything can be bigger. Plan for large construction – use huge boxes, massive cardboard tubes, big bricks – all contributing to experiences involving weight.
- Play games involving children positioning themselves behind, on top and so on encourages mathematical language

Knowledge and Understanding of the World

To foster in a child a sense of excitement and the sheer joy of finding something out is a rewarding experience. The world is out there for them and although you cannot provide all the answers you can make it so they want to find out more. You need to plan carefully and provide the means for them but not give the answers. The outdoor environment for some children is magical when they can dig and find a worm, or if they are playing with the bubbles in water.

- Plan for play that is open ended, so there is no answer but lots of questions. For example, what is the snail doing on the wall? Does it live there? What happens to bubbles? Where do they go?
- Plan for children to be investigators – what is under the log pile today?
- Plan for them to plant seeds, watch them grow, measure them, see what happens when they die and to experiment with them.
- Plan for them to take on the roles of others such as shopkeeper, doctor, garage mechanic and, with expert adult support, learn how to deal with difficult customers and situations.
- Plan for the children to be outside in all weathers – with appropriate clothing of course. They can learn so much about changing weather patterns, what it feels like to walk on slippery frost or be out in the wind.
- Plan for the children to try building constructions from different materials. The outdoor area is ideal for putting up tepees, huts, creating dens and caves.

Physical Development

Children up to five years old are starting to learn control and develop their movement skills. You can help them to gain greater control by providing them with opportunities to explore and experiment with body movement. To do this they need to acquire essential skills.

- Balance – developing coordination and control of body actions. Plan to develop these by providing equipment and games: walking along chalk lines on the floor, rope pathways, small balancing beams, stepping stones, building using large equipment, carrying heavier objects.

- Locomotion – focusing on basic motor skills such as running, jumping and moving the body around in different ways. Games such as 'Cat and mouse', 'What's the time Mr Wolf?', 'Simon says' all promote development of these skills and could be planned.
- Manipulative skills – using equipment to develop the techniques of aiming, predicting and estimating. Planning for these skills could involve throwing balls into containers or through hoops.

Plan to allow children time to explore and develop large pieces of equipment so that they are initiating their own movements and creating their own challenges. These need not be a climbing frame but could be large boxes, planks of wood, drainpipes and plastic crates. Are there plenty of safe mirrors outside so that children can see their body shape in the space? Plan for experiences that allow children to use a range of small and large equipment safely.

Creative Development

What gives us pleasure in our lives today? It may be reading a good book, listening to music, enjoying a painting, going to the cinema or theatre or dancing. We don't all enjoy the same things but we appreciate the ways other people are able to express their thoughts and ideas.

When planning for creative development outdoors you need to provide many varied experiences - it is not just taking the painting easel outside! Children are naturally curious and if within their environment there are things for them to touch, feel and smell they will do so.

- Plan for the children to have access to a variety of artefacts, including ones for the outdoor area. Maybe set up a pottery workshop outside and the children can model to add to the collection.
- Provide materials so the children can respond to others but are also able to create for themselves. Outside the children can do this without fear of making a mess. They can experiment with different materials and on

various textures. Plan for the resources to be available so that the children can make choices. It is unrealistic to suggest that the children have unlimited choice of unlimited resources but sometimes they are restricted in what they are able to do because we only provide them with paints and large sheets of white paper.

- Plan for the children to have access to music and different sound making outside. This is the ideal place for it! There are many outdoor musical instruments available now and it is easy to set up a sound workshop in a corner outside. The children can experiment with many materials, finding out for example what sound is made when a length of chain is dropped down a plastic tube.
- Plan for an area where the children can dance to music or perform if that is something they like to do. Provide them with streamers or ribbons and a tape recorder with a variety of music.
- Many children can be creative through role play and storytelling and if you provide the means for this the rewards are tremendous.

One of the most important points to consider when thinking about imaginative play is time. If children are aware that they will soon have to come away from the imaginative play area more often than not their play will not be focused and of a high quality. It is far better for them to know that they will have time and for staff to expect children to take ownership of the area to develop their play. The area has to be as well resourced as possible and to suit as many varieties of imaginative play as possible. It needs to accommodate children to be able to cooperate with each other, negotiate, share and discuss, so if it is too small an area these skills will not be developed. The equipment can be on a much larger scale than indoors - things like various sizes of wood, large tubes, pieces of carpet, tree trunks, wheeled vehicles, prams and bikes (see pages 19-23 for advice on resources). Prop boxes should be developed with quality items – real objects. Clothes and accessories promote quality play.

Sometimes you can set up an imaginative area in the same way that you do indoors. This can be particularly successful if time and thought has followed a period of observations.

One group may well be playing for some considerable period and you, as the observing adult, can see how to extend their play by producing a forest area for monsters, for example. This may not be possible until the next day but often children will play the same games over and over because you have inspired and extended their play.

The difference with the outdoor fantasy area is there is much more scope for large movement and noisy play and it involves the whole child.

As you can see, planning could be a complicated business. How can you plan for the children to have all of these experiences all at once? Well, of course, you can't and you wouldn't want them to. What you need to do is observe them all the time and plan for where you think they are going. Most early years settings organise their year around themes that the children are familiar with and then try to extend the skills of the children through the theme so that it means something to the children in their everyday lives. In that way children are interested.

Example planning sheet for outdoor play

Theme: Homes/families

Areas of Learning	What are the children learning?	Key Questions/ Starting Points	Other related activities
Personal, Social and Emotional	Are they becoming increasingly independent in selecting activities? Do they understand the inside/outside routine?	What do I see on my way to school? The Three Little Pigs story Harvest time	The Three Little Pigs story? Large bricks/small bricks for construction Sand play – making roads
Communication, Language and Literacy	Do they listen to and join in with stories? Are they beginning to handle books correctly? Can they sequence a story? Are they aware of some simple rhyming words?	**Adult led activities** Map of journey to school 'Blow paintings Digging and planting bulbs	Water play – blowing bubbles Small world – Role playThe Three Little Pigs story
Problem Solving, Reasoning and Numeracy	Can the children count up to 10? Can they recognise numbers 1,2,3? Do the children know first, second, third?	Number line – counting to 5	Drawing Outdoor kit bag (creatures)
Creative Development	Can the children talk about the colours they are using? Can they tap out some simple rhythms?	'Listening' walk	Re-enacting The Three Little Pigs story in the role-play area?
Physical Development	Do the children respond to 'stop' and 'go'? Are they aware of giving others their personal space?	**Possible group activities** Introduce harvest song Count to 10, and solve problems orally	Planting daffodil bulbs
Knowledge and Understanding of the World	Do the children show an interest in their family? Can they talk about them? Do they notice what they pass on their way to school?	Five little ducks, Five autumn leaves On my way to school song	**Outdoors** Mon am pm Tues am pm Wed **Forest School** Thurs am pm Fri am pm
Special Events	Introduce Harvest time Do the children have a knowledge of some common vegetables?	Vegetable bag Rhythm – tapping sticks	

Observation template for weekly outdoor play

Areas of Learning	What am I looking for?
Personal, Social and Emotional	Are children becoming increasingly independent in selecting activities?
	Do they understand the inside/outside routine?
Communication, Language and Literacy	Do they listen to and join in with stories?
	Are they beginning to handle books correctly?
	Can they sequence a story?
	Are they aware of some simple rhyming words?
Problem Solving, Reasoning and Numeracy	Can the children count up to 10?
	Can they recognise numbers 1,2,3?
	Do the children know first, second, third?
Creative Development	Can the children talk about the colours they are using?
	Can they tap out some simple rhythms?
Physical Development	Do the children respond to 'stop' and 'go'?
	Are they aware of giving others their personal space?
Knowledge and Understanding of the World	Do the children show an interest in their family? Can they talk about it?
	Do they notice what they pass on their way to school?

Areas of Learning	What am I looking for?
Personal, Social and Emotional	Add your comments here.
Communication, Language and Literacy	
Problem Solving, Reasoning and Numeracy	
Creative Development	
Physical Development	
Knowledge and Understanding of the World	

Outdoor Play

Outside areas can be too big, too small, too sprawled, not enough grass. They may not have direct access to the indoors, they may not have shade, they may never receive the sun. Whatever is available will affect the children's learning and you must make the best of whatever there is.

When designing the area the needs of the children must be paramount. Sometimes this is difficult if the senior management or the people who hold the purse strings are not convinced of the power of outdoor learning. One common costly mistake is installing impressive adventure playground equipment that takes up a huge amount of space and can limit the learning potential for the children. Fixed equipment can sometimes be a problem if it hasn't been planned properly. Where to site it is crucial. Before attempting to design the layout, look at:

● What access do you have from inside to outside?
● What size is your area?
● What fixed equipment do you already have?
● What surfaces do you have?

Access

There are many ways that children can move from one area to another. The simplest and the most effective is to have doors leading from the indoor to the outdoor area so the children can move freely between them. However, in many settings the doors also have to accommodate parents and carers as this may be the only way in, and this can have implications for security and monitoring who comes and goes. The outdoor area may be the place where parents gather to wait in the mornings to see their children enter safely. If equipment is left outside at this time it may be moved or even damaged, albeit not deliberately. It may be possible to spend some time with the parents explaining your intentions about setting up the outdoor area for learning, and in this way they will begin to understand and appreciate the importance of it for their child.

What can be done to help?

● Set up a removable fence around the area – and quickly readjust later.
● Make an alleyway through the area by using some kind of fencing/bollards.
● Set up the equipment and cover it with cloth/ tarpaulin – this can often detract from the activity and says 'Please don't touch yet'.
● Put small removable objects into boxes or containers until later when it can be finally set up.

The size of the area

No matter what size your outdoor area there are always difficulties with this. If it is too small, children will become frustrated because they won't be able to run around without knocking others over. Run-around games may have to be organised in another way – perhaps even using the space once it has been cleared of equipment.

What can be done to make sure a small outdoor area is used effectively?

■ Use the area as you would any other part of your setting, such as the construction or creative area. Children will learn quickly that four children only can dig in the pots or six children play in the imaginary play area.
● Make sure you offer the broad mix of activities and experiences needed by carefully observing the children and then planning for the outdoor area with these in mind. If the children need lots of opportunities for being creative at this time, dispense with other areas of learning and resource the area to enhance their creativity. For example, provide lots of imaginary materials, take in collections, provide large sheets of paper, paints, allow them space to dramatise, let them make music. If their priority is communication or literacy the resources you provide should reflect this.
● Make sure that the whole area is used, including the fence and walls.

- Do not allow the outdoor area to become a place for storing surplus furniture!
- If the physical play or practising small skills such as using balls and hoops has to be organised because of lack of space, do make sure this is carried out systematically and on a regular basis otherwise teaching points will have been lost.
- Dispense with bikes! They are not essential and do need a lot of space. The same skills can be practised using other resources.
- Digging and gardening can still be offered but possibly using a rota system. There are many types of containers that can be used for holding soil, bulb fibre or bark. Plant and observe seeds and plants. Build a log pile - it doesn't take long for the insects and minibeasts to find it.

What if you have a large outdoor space? Some children find it difficult to settle in a large space and will flit from one activity to another – it almost becomes a playground environment.

- If at all possible have an area that is yours alone. Often large spaces are shared by several groups of children and it is difficult to plan the activities if another group of children is going to use them as well. It might also be worth considering marking off an area in some way for each group of children, even though the areas will be much smaller. The quality of play is likely to be raised.
- Break up a large area by dividing it into sections. There could be sections for physical play, for quiet solitary play, for imaginary play, for construction/engineering type play, and so on. This could be done with seating and hedges, by using removable fencing panels, or even chalking lines on the floor.
- Avoid taking on a supervisory role, as often happens in a large area. For best play, adults should be interacting with children.

Fixed equipment
- If equipment is already fixed in your area there is little you can do about it – just work around it. There may be ways that you could extend the learning potential of

the equipment, such as using blankets and sheets to make a den underneath.
- If you have little or no fixed equipment then you have a versatile and flexible area to work with. By providing the children with lots of large movable equipment that they have control over, their play is greatly improved because they need to think about what they want the equipment to be and where to place it.
- Many settings buy playhouse structures/sheds to use as their imaginary play area and provide excellent resources in the form of prop boxes to enhance them, but they can take up quite a lot of valuable space. Often the same quality of play can be found using cardboard boxes and blankets with the prop boxes - sometimes even better! The playhouse can be used for other purposes – perhaps to read quietly, to use as a gardening/potting shed/for scientific experiments.
- One fixed structure that is valuable is a large sandpit. Children can then get into it with their socks off and feel the sand between their toes. It can be filled with something other than sand at different times of the year, such as leaves, logs or water. It should be covered over to prevent animals from fouling in it. If the cover is wooden and strong enough the children can use it as a stage. Again, careful consideration needs to be taken as to where to site it.

Surfaces

For the outdoor area to be as effective as possible it should have a variety of surfaces:

- Hard standing for general games, wheeled vehicles (if necessary) and for standing tables or pieces of other lightweight equipment. It is best for the hard standing to be immediately outside the doors so that the children do not take in mud or grass with them as they go in and out
- Grassy area with a slope or hill for rolling would be ideal. Grassy areas are best for sitting and placing small gym equipment.
- Textured area such as pebbles, gravel or tiles. Textured areas are ideal for becoming the quieter areas where children can have sensory experiences.

To have all these surfaces in one setting is ideal but if all you have is tarmac there are ways and means of providing experiences for the children by using a little ingenuity. You can provide a piece of carpet for the children to sit on or put textured tiles along the walls or fencing. If you have only grass it would be worth taking some of it up and replacing with tarmac. If used constantly, grass does become worn and muddy and even if the children have wellies it can become slippery if not well maintained. If you have a small area of tarmac at least the children can still go outside even on the rainiest of days!

The design of the outdoor area

If the area is to be interesting for children it should incorporate different levels as well as surfaces. If at all possible have a slope for the children to run and roll down. It needn't be huge or even that steep. See if any parents can donate house bricks and make a wiggly path through the grass for the children to follow. Is there somewhere for you to install a stile for the children to climb over to get to another area? (better than a gate) Can you put an archway through to your quiet story corner or make a maze from hedging or wooden posts?

Is there a wall in your area that you can paint as the backdrop to a favourite scenario - a garage, café, garden centre? Can you screw some hooks into it so that you can hang up signs, washing lines, or place batons along the wall so that you can have some drop-down surfaces when you want them?

Safety and risk assessment

Staff always consider safety and risk whenever they have children in their care, whether inside or outside. When the children are outside it could be argued that there is a greater element of risk because they are most likely to be engaged in physical activity of some description. Good practice in safety should be of paramount importance and all staff should be aware of what is and what isn't good practice.

How do you make sure the outside area is safe?

- Make a quick daily check that the resources being used that day are in good working order:
  Check for splinters in wood
  Wipe metal equipment after rain
  Make sure the equipment has been securely put together
- Check the ground for glass, litter, or unwanted items that may have been left by overnight visitors.
- When equipment has been assembled, make sure it is at the correct height with no pieces jutting out at child level.
- Make sure that children do not behave in a dangerous way. Always be alert to those children who haven't yet reached a high level of understanding of the possibilities of danger with some of the activities put out for them.
- Teach the children to use the equipment correctly from the start so taking away some potential for accidents.
- Make sure the children know that some of them can do things that others can't yet, for example climb high on the frame.

- Produce guidelines and teach the children rules about not pushing and pulling each other.
- Do not allow vehicles and other apparatus to be left under climbing frames.
- Children should climb only with appropriate footwear and never while wearing long flowing clothing.
- Rubber tyres are great fun but should not be rolled around, unless with adult help.

Risk assessments should be carried out before every outdoor session. They only take a few minutes to complete but are essential. It is about looking at the materials that are available for the children and making sure they are placed safely. It is vital if the area is small to make sure that the doorway is uncluttered. Where the children get the equipment from and how is another element of risk assessment. Settings are now required to produce a risk assessment document telling staff and parents about the safety measures put into place for their children and it is good practice to complete simple sheets every day as a record.

A word of warning! Although you must make every effort to make sure children are safe from danger, you cannot and should not be taking away the element of risk that is present in good outdoor practice. Children need challenge and are stimulated by some risk taking. If everything they do is safe they will not bother to see if they can jump a little higher, or be a little faster. You need to be providing them with challenges that seem risky to them, and if they fail it doesn't matter because you are there for support. Children will rarely do anything that feels unsafe to them but will take a risk if ably supported.

The role of adults

The interaction between adults and children is vital. You are not there to act as supervisor but as someone who furthers play situations by producing a piece of equipment or prop at the right time by ensuring that some children do not dominate or by just asking the right qestions and

being. It is about making sure that all children have choices, encouraging them to try out new skills and ideas.

When children are using the outdoor environment the adults will be working with them. At the same time they will be observing and assessing the children's learning exactly the same as when indoors. Just by working outside with the children you are raising the profile and status of the outside area not just in the eyes of the children but also their parents. (Often outdoor play is seen as of secondary importance to parents - the children are not learning, just playing!)

Where indoor and outdoor play are happening at the same time a member of staff should be in each area. This needs to be flexible. It might be that the member of staff outside is involved in a play situation that the children want to carry on indoors and is needed there. In that case the staff need to be aware of this and allow another staff member to be outside.

If you rely a lot on voluntary helpers/parents/carers it is vital that they understand from the outset the value of the play and the activities you have prepared for the children. Some helpers are excellent at playing with the children and are a real asset to the children's learning and without their help children may not be able to go outside at all.

The most important issue to remember is that when adults are interacting with children in a sensitive way, whether inside or outside, the quality of the learning is improved. So often adults are seen supervising and sorting out conflict rather than intervening and enabling the play to continue by providing the next steps.

Helping the children begin their play outside is often an important role for the adult. Stories are an ideal way to introduce a theme for outdoor play and an imaginative storyteller can inspire wonderful play. Gathering resources for the play is another vital role and most parents are helpful if they are asked beforehand to bring certain items in. Many settings provide a broad outline of their planned themes and either through newsletters or, better still, through their constant day-to-day contact, the parents know what the play is likely to involve that term and are only too pleased to be part of it. In this way, you can spread the message of the importance of outdoor play.

Systems and routines

Children need to know what is expected of them and what to expect from others. Routines are important so that they can operate at as independent a level as possible. What can you do to enable children to become independent?

- Make sure they understand when they can go outside:
  Any time – they can choose;
  With their group – at a given time;
  With a group chosen at random.
- Choose a system that suits your group:
  Put their name on a Velcro strip by the door;
  Put their name in a tub;
  Take a coloured band that is displayed by the door (perhaps limiting the number - eight bands means eight children outside);
  Write their names on a board, clipboard or in a book

with thin or thick felts, pencils, chalks or whatever is appropriate or available.
Have photos of children which they can move.

- Make sure the children know where and how to get their coats and wellies and how to store them afterwards:
  If possible, have the coats kept near the door to the outside;
  Have a shelf/pocket for each child's shoes/wellies;
  Keep a wellie box with a carpet by the door so the children can change their boots quickly;
  Have coloured pegs so the boots can be paired up and transfer the pegs to the shoes so they can be found quickly;
  Make a wooden strip with cut lengths of broom handles in twos and slot the wellies upside down;
  Paint the toes of pairs of wellies so they match.

Outside in all weathers

The British weather doesn't often lend itself to prolonged outdoor play. It can be too cold, too hot, too rainy, too windy. However, children will often still choose to go outside whatever the weather and we can sometimes be in danger of missing a valuable learning experience if we keep them inside.

Coats and wellies, warm gloves and hats should be available at all times for the cold and wet weather.

- Sun hats should be provided for hot weather.
- Willow structures can provide welcome shade and can be planted in any form - tunnels, tents and igloos.
- Bought canopies are cheap and easy to assemble.
- More solid structures such as verandahs are ideal.
- Pergolas with planting around or across the top provide shade.
- Trees and shrubs can provide excellent shelter, as can make-shift tents and canopies, large parasols (no good in windy weather!) and windbreaks.

Some outdoor areas are excellent in that the children have some sun and some shade, but others have to contend with continual shade or wind. It can be difficult for staff to be motivated if they know they have to be outside in the wind all morning and the quality of the play can be affected by the weather, so care has to be taken about what to provide for the children. There is no easy answer but common sense has to prevail and if the sun is too hot the children will need to be indoors unless some form of shelter is available to them.

Assessing children's progress

With all of the activities described some of the children will achieve an outcome, others will dabble and appear to not accomplish the task, whilst there will be those who are not interested in the activity at all! How do you keep track? Know your children!

When they first enter your setting you will have talked at length to the parents to find out what their child is interested in and begin to have an insight into their learning style. You will have notes about this. If they have come to you from a pre-school setting you will have spoken to the previous provider and formed some idea of what motivates that particular child.

When planning for the week's activities outside, deciding what learning experiences you think should be next in their development, you must take account of the differences in their learning styles. For example, the learning intention might be to enable the children to be aware of 3-d shape. Some children will learn this concept through building with large solid shapes, others might need to wrap the shape in large sheets of paper, others will paint them (cover them with paint), arrange them in patterns, put them in bags or use them in role play. Your intention stays the same but the way in which you help children to understand the concept will change.

During the week you might write notes about significant happenings related to the learning intention, and stick them on the outside planning sheet. When you plan for the following week you can then take account of the comments made and include a 'next step' if necessary. You must be realistic when planning for progress and be sure to take account of what the children already know – be ready to challenge them always. It is not good enough to just send them out on their trikes to let off steam. They can use the trikes to go around an obstacle course made of large 3-d shapes! 'Can you get to the cube shape without knocking anything over?' 'Go around the large ball shape, the sphere, and come back to me!'

Assessing children need not be complicated. Be focused on what you are looking for and only take notes about that. In that way you will do it on a regular basis and will be able to see the progress the children are making.

When deciding what the learning intentions for the week are going to be, make sure they are spread over the six areas of learning and not too heavily biased towards the literacy and numeracy strands. All six areas have equal importance!

When children and adults are outside they will need furniture and a variety of resources. The furniture will mainly be seating in some form, storage of some kind and perhaps some surfaces for the children to work on.

Seating

Whether seating is available can influence quite considerably how children play. It is daunting to some children if they can't sit sometimes and adults need to be able to sit down occasionally. It should be as varied as possible, for example:
- Bought benches – often need to be fixed to the ground so are permanent
- Crates and planks
- Wooden stepping stone type
- Large tyres
- Cut tree trunks
- Receptacles such as wooden boxes and plastic trays
- The non-permanent type of seating is useful for demarcating areas outdoors, for example separating the physical play area from the quieter area.

Storage

Make the storage of equipment and resources as child-friendly as possible, for example:
- Movable storage trolleys for awkward pieces of apparatus, such as drainpipe cut-offs, pieces of tubing, lengths of wood, chains, ropes, 'engineering' equipment, measuring sticks, hose pipes.
- Plastic shopping baskets that can hold sets of cups, cutlery or clothing that can be hung up.
- Nets that can hold balls of various sizes, bean bags or hats that can be hung up.
- Boxes on wheels for each type of resource, for example gardening, scientific, water, small world.
- Plastic crates that can be stacked.
- Vegetable rack type of storage for smaller equipment such as magnifying glasses, collecting boxes, spoons for digging, markers.

- A storage shed that is properly organised so the children can access equipment with supervision – with hooks at child height so they can be encouraged to hang nets up.
- Provide seating that can double up as storage space, for example with lift-up lids or space underneath.

Surfaces

The children will often need a work top to gather around or use as a collecting point. This could be:

- A picnic bench
- A table brought from inside
- Crates with sheets of wood laid across them
- A piece of carpet
- An upturned box
- A wallpapering trestle (with legs shortened) for collaborative painting/collage

Basic requirements

All of the resources listed below are basic. They are categorised under each area of learning and development, but many could easily be in all areas.

Personal, Social and Emotional Development

The children are beginning to learn about who they are and how they feel about the others around them. The resources need to reflect this and give them opportunities to become others. They need to experiment with their feelings so sensory equipment is important.

Assortment of clothing:
- Dresses, long and glamorous
- Trousers, dungarees
- Tops, cloaks
- Hats, helmets
- Sunglasses and glasses with clear frames
- Shoes, boots (workman type)
- Scarves and pieces of material, feather boas
- Handbags, shopping bags, purses with real money

Basic home equipment:
- Crockery, cutlery, kitchen utensils, phone
- Cardboard boxes can be used for large equipment such as cooker
- Blankets, sheets, cushions, pieces of carpet

Assortment of toys:
- Dolls, teddies, animals
- Tents
- Outdoor mirror
- Textured surfaces such as sandpaper, mosaic, marble, cement
- Scrubbing brushes

Communication, Language and Literacy

Resourcing for this area of learning is about enabling the children to communicate with each other in a variety of forms.

- Collaborative table or work area
- Sandpit/mud tray/water tray
- Construction equipment
- Quiet place for reading/telling stories/collection of books
- Blackboards/whiteboards/clipboards
- Tray with assorted papers for writing and drawing
- Tray with variety of writing implements - chalks, paintbrushes, pencils, pens, sticks
- Variety of letter shapes - wooden, plastic, cards with letters, name cards
- Telephones, notepads, sticky tape, staplers, glue, scissors
- Prop boxes for drama, in other words planned stories that you intend encouraging the children to role play with. These can include clothing, accessories and props such as masks for retelling the chosen stories, for example 'Goldilocks', 'The Three Pigs' (see page 21).

Problem Solving, Reasoning and Numeracy

Think about providing opportunities for the children to count, keep score of a game, make patterns using shapes, and use the vocabulary of maths such as 'heavy', 'light', 'more' or 'less'.

- Wooden bricks and tiles
- Variety of pipes, ropes, lengths of sticks for ordering
- Large and small cardboard boxes, tubes
- Laminated number cards, large and small numbers
- Carpet tiles
- Collecting dishes for counting things out and in
- Measuring sticks, tape measures
- Stepping stones with numbers painted on them
- Masking tape for making number grids/ladders
- Hoops and embroidery rings
- Balls, buckets and bean bags for throwing and counting games

Knowledge and Understanding of the World

Children are constantly enquiring about things around them and need opportunities to be able to take time to look in depth at some of the things they find. They need to be able to 'see what happens if' and so there should be lots of resources around them to encourage them to do just that.

- Pile of logs or old piece of carpet for gathering minibeasts
- Sink/box/tray for keeping water beasts in
- Collecting pots, magnifying glasses, small nets, clipboards, pencils
- Reference books, digital camera and small video cameras
- Bird table, bird box, bird bath
- Bubble blowers, kites, rain collectors
- Gardening tools, for example trowels, watering cans, hose, canes, wheelbarrow, flower pots, plastic containers for digging in, or buckets and bowls
- Containers for a herb garden
- Plastic crates, planks, plastic tubing, guttering, funnels, piping
- Collections of stones, twigs, leaves, bark, cork, bottle tops, pieces of wood

Physical Development

Flexibility is the all-important word. Equipment that can be moved around and used imaginatively whilst engaging the children in an abundance of physical activity is vital, and fairly cheap to organise.

- Blocks – large and small, heavy and light
- Wooden and plastic crates
- Large cardboard boxes
- Tyres
- Tree trunks
- Climbing frame
- Balancing planks
- Cones
- Tunnel
- Ropes
- Ladder

Creative Development

To allow children to be creative you need to give them the space and tools - they don't need anything else! If they see musical instruments they will try them out!

- Large space where paper can be fixed to a wall or fence for painting/collage and brushes, sticks, pens, chalks and paints
- Large wooden blocks
- Assortment of shells, leaves, sticks, small pebbles, long grasses, twigs with a variety of card, paper, frames to enable the children to make pictures
- Props to enable dramatic play, for example masks, swatches of material, blankets
- Music-making prop box – shells, flower pots, small musical instruments such as maracas, shakers, tambourines, chimes and bells and larger ones such as drums, large xylophone, chimes

If you are thinking of extending your resources, here are some suggestions:

- Small table and chairs for imaginative play
- Tablecloth, parasol, small stand-alone blackboards for menus
- Hat stand for hanging notices as well as clothes
- Wheeled vehicles such as bikes, trucks and prams that can take more than one child
- Trailers, trolleys and carts that can be pushed and pulled independently
- Wheelbarrow, grow-bags, small cloche, seed trays
- Collection of fossils and archaeological artefacts for burying and finding
- Herb garden planted in a box or old sink
- Bird boxes, wormery and small animal area (rabbits, guinea pigs), incubator for hatching eggs
- Weather station and fun mobiles
- Different kinds of balls, spikey balls, heavy and light balls
- Small and large hoops
- Different-sized bean bags
- Parachute
- Aiming games such as soft darts
- Netball posts
- Climbing nets
- Woodwork area including a tree trunk with mallet and nails
- Sculpting area using clay
- Large construction materials such as large Meccano
- Real building bricks, tree slices, stones and rocks
- Barrels and drums for extending physical play
- Tarpaulins, large blankets and camouflage netting
- Hose pipes and industrial tubing
- Guttering and an assortment of plastic buckets
- Canopies, pergolas, large umbrellas
- Outdoor mirror
- Swaying bridge, slides and concrete tunnels

Prop boxes

Prop boxes are a good way to organise and plan for the outdoors. Although the smaller items are kept in the box, the larger items that are used time and time again are

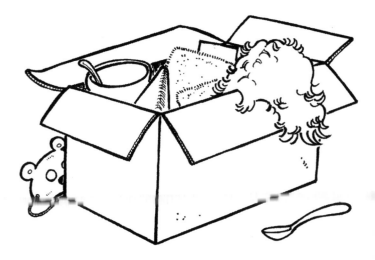

included in the scene. There are several types. They can be used for:

- Re-enacting stories
- Setting a scene
- To support specific activities

Re-enacting stories

The Three Little Pigs – could be linked with the themes of Materials, Homes, Journeys, Animals, Number three.
The box could include masks of the animals (mother pig, three pigs, wolf), carpet/carpet tiles to denote the old house, dusters or cloths and an apron, three cardboard boxes with straw, twigs and bricks with which to make the houses (flatten them out), a box or something similar for the chimney for the wolf to climb into; and the story book. Also some laminated signs that can be hooked up in the play area, for example 'The pigs' house', 'The house of sticks', 'I'll huff and I'll puff and I'll blow your house down'.

Goldilocks and the Three Bears – could be linked to the themes of Number three, Sizes, Journeys, Food.
The box could include the masks for the bears, a golden (blonde) wig, some trees (cones, posts), three bowls, three spoons, porridge oats, three small stools/chairs, three pieces of carpet (beds), a cover for Goldilocks and a version

of the story. Some laminated signs could include '1, 2, 3', 'The three bears' cottage', and the song 'When Goldilocks went to the house of the bears'.

Jack and the Beanstalk – could be linked with the themes of Homes (castles), Opposites (big and little), Growth. The box could include a large cardboard box, a long rope, some pebbles, a packet of seeds, some large shoes and the storybook. Laminated signs could include 'Giant's castle', 'The beanstalk', 'Fe Fi Fo Fum I smell the blood of an Englishman'.

Cinderella – could be linked with the themes of Fairy tales, Magic, Clothes (shoes), Homes (castles), Time. The box could include some ugly masks, an assortment of shoes, a pretty shoe, dresses and jewellery, a mirror, a clock, a large cardboard box and a version of the story. Laminated signs could include 'The ugly sisters', 'The carriage', '12 o'clock midnight'.

Hansel and Gretel – could be linked with Food, Journeys. The box could include a large box, some cones, a bag of pebbles, a witch's outfit, a long rope, some tubs filled with ginger for the smell and the story on tape or book. Laminated signs could include 'The gingerbread house', 'The forest' and 'Hansel and Gretel'.

Noah's Ark – could be linked with Water, Weather, Number two, Journeys, Animals, Floating and sinking, Rainbows and Light. The box could include a large box, animal masks (in twos), some building tools such as hammer, nails, planks of wood, aprons, buckets and the story. Laminated signs could include 'The ark', 'Noah', 'The mountain', the song 'The animals went in two by two'.

We're going on a bear hunt – could be linked with Journeys, Sounds, Animals, Friends. The box could include a large box, some smaller flattened out boxes, a blanket, some blue material, teddy, long grasses or ribbons and the song and book We're Going on a Bear Hunt. Laminated signs could indicate some of the obstacles they meet along the way: 'The river', 'The mud', 'The long grass' and, of course, 'The bear'.

Setting a scene

These are prop boxes that give children the starting point for their imaginary play. The list is endless but here are some proven, successful scenarios that are especially good for outside.

The café/ restaurant - could be linked with the themes of Food, Healthy eating, a special country, using money Tablecloth, china, utensils, small wipe-off board for menu, small notebooks and pads for the orders and bills, telephone, aprons and cloths. Laminated signs for 'Café open', 'Closed', 'Please wait to be seated', 'No smoking'.

The take-away/fast food restaurant – could be linked with the themes of Food, Journeys, the local environment, Transport. Telephones, notepads, supply of boxes for the food, delivery vehicles, some laminated numbers and addresses, a bag for the hot food box, crash helmet and safety bib.

The garage and service centre – could be linked with Transport and Wheels. Assortment of tools for mending the vehicles, mechanics' dungarees, bunches of keys, notepads, telephone, old tyres and cardboard inspection ramp. Laminated signs for 'Garage', MOT sign, 'Danger', 'No smoking'.

Garden centre - linked with the themes of Growth, Plants, using money. Flower pots and tubs, bulb fibre, seed packets, plastic flowers, baskets, gardening tools, aprons, hose pipe/watering cans, sand and gravel, wheelbarrow, till and money. Laminated signs for plant area, building materials, signs for prices of flowers and plants.

The camp site - linked with Homes, Holidays, Journeys, Travel. More than one tent – preferably four/five, airbeds, blankets, buckets and water carriers, fold-up chairs, cooking equipment and implements. Laminated signs for camp site, shower block, toilets and shop.

The airport – linked with Transport, Flight, Journeys, Shape, Counting. Uniforms, tickets, luggage of various sorts and sizes, trolleys, conveyer belt made from corrugated card, x-ray machine made from a box, café area and television screen with destination. Laminated signs such as 'Entrance', 'Exit', 'Taxis', gate numbers, 'Baggage reclaim'

The theme park – linked with Holidays. Ticket booth, tickets, credit cards, café area, an assortment of rides, for example trailer ride around a prepared pathway, an obstacle course made up of going under blankets, through tunnels, balancing along a plank and aiming games with a prize for the highest number. Laminated signs for theme park, ticket booth, prices, café, menus and prices, entrance and exit, names of rides, 'Queue here'.

Builders' yard – links with Homes, Materials. As many real materials as possible - bricks, breeze blocks, planks and assorted pieces of wood, guttering and drain pipes, ropes and buckets, spades, wheelbarrow, helmets and dungarees, larger transport vehicles such as dump trucks, lorries, cement mixers, sand and water and cones. Laminated signs such as 'Danger', 'Men at work', 'Hard hats must be worn at all times'.

The beach – links with Holidays. Beachwear such as swimming costumes, towels, sunglasses, sun hats, parasol, beach chairs, flippers, snorkelling masks, airbeds, a sand pit to climb into or an area with sand, pebbles, buckets and spades, fishing nets, a paddling pool with water, an ice cream shop, a café, cases, beach bags, rucksacks. Laminated signs such as 'Shop', 'Ice cream for sale', prices board.

An outdoor concert – links with music, dance and drama. Some costumes and jewellery, tickets, a microphone, some guitars, drums and other musical instruments. A stage area could be slightly raised from the floor using planks and bricks, seating for the audience, café area or hotdog stand. Laminated signs such as 'Ticket booth', 'Entrance' and 'Exit', 'Hot dogs', prices board.

The desert island – links with Journeys, Treasure, Water, Transport. Large sandy coloured rug to represent the island, blue kite fabric as the sea, parasol and stand, swimming

costumes, sun glasses, collection of plastic creatures, for example crabs, fish, sharks, fishing nets, driftwood, hammock, stones and shells, bottles, writing implements and paper (charcoal), logs and planks for raft construction.

Activity prop boxes

These are boxes of equipment to place outside for children who want to pursue a particular activity, perhaps individually or in pairs. They would not always be available but when they are they must be fully resourced with a prompt card explaining for any adult the purpose of the box and how it could be used.

The treasure hunt
In the box will be a prepared list of objects (this could be in picture form) for the children to go and find. It could be on a theme, for example items from a story, numbers, letters, or a variety of objects for the children to find in the garden.

Snails
This only works if the area has some stone walling or a suitable snail environment! Include a collecting box for

looking at the captured snail, a magnifying glass, some paper on a clipboard for the children to draw the pattern of the snail shell if they wish, a book about snails.

Minibeasts
Some collecting boxes with lids, magnifying glasses, minibeast picture books, a small trowel, some paper for drawing on a clipboard, a digital camera if possible.

Fossils/archaeology
Prepare a piece of ground or box with earth in which are placed some fossils or other items of archaeological interest, such as pieces of tiles or china. The children look for these items. In their box will be a collecting tray, a small trowel, some small brushes for cleaning their precious items, some paper for recording their finds.

Colour palette
The colour cards from DIY stores are a good starting point. Cut them into strips according to colour range. Ask the children to find objects that closely match the blocks in the colour chart. They might find leaves, grasses, fir cones or pieces of paper, a toy, an item of clothing. Once they have found some you can ask them to display their items in the same order or hang them on a washing line.

Rubbings
A rubbings box can be made up of a variety of materials. These could include different types of papers, crayons, charcoals. The children have to find the surfaces to rub and perhaps provide a display of their finds. A game can be played whereby other children have to spot where the particular rubbing was made – the wall, the side of the climbing frame, the tree. Alternatively, you prepare a set of rubbings for the children to spot. They will need to look closely at the outside area to see the patterns.

Sketching
This box can be filled with a variety of notepads, sketch books, files, pencils, colouring pens, charcoal and chalks so that the children are not restricted in what media they choose to use for their drawings. Sometimes they may like

to use a frame and only draw what is inside the frame. This activity works well if it is modelled by an adult so they are working alongside the children at their own sketching.

Measuring
Fill a box with all kinds of measuring implements – different lengths of string, ropes, tape measures of different types, long pieces of rolled card, pencils, height charts, hands and feet prints, box of paper-clips for measuring smaller items.

Collage/mobiles
This box would enable a child or group to make a collage picture. Include sheets of different paper, large and small, frames for weaving, glue, cloth or fabric, wire coat-hangers, string, wire and cutters. Encourage the children to use natural materials for their collage.

Activities to support Personal, Social and Emotional Develoment

Soapy sand

What do you want the children to learn or develop or develop or develop

Seek and delight and have a positive approach to new experiences

Linked areas of learning

Communication, Language and Literacy
Knowledge and Understanding of the World

Themed links

The beach, Senses, Materials

Resources

Shallow tray
Deep bucket
Assorted sand, wet and dry
Containers with washing-up liquid
Cups, bottles, tubes, jugs, spoons, funnels, stirrers
Things with holes, such as sieves and colanders
Sand wheels
Flour, clay
Salt
Pebbles, lentils, peas and beans

Provide a variety of shallow and deep containers, some sand and a variety of equipment to experiment with. As this is a messy activity, have plenty of plastic sheeting available, and easy access for washing and drying hands.

Ask the children: 'What happens to the sand if you put liquid into it?' Encourage them to experiment with adding liquids such as water and then washing-up liquid, so that it is smooth to touch.

Make a mixture of dry sand and clay to make it gritty. Mix together lentils, beans and peas with sand and add water. Let the children handle the materials and experience their different properties. Some children will want to try pouring and filling containers, others will be happy just to feel the sand between their fingers. If you have children who don't like getting messy, encourage them to join in but let them stand and watch as much as they want. Maybe they can add a small piece to something you have made. Let them know where they can wash their hands - perhaps even put a bowl of water close by.

- Challenge the children to make some small delicate things as well as mixing.
- Help them to describe the materials using words such as 'rough', 'sticky', 'crumbly'.
- Allow the children time just to experiment themselves without having to make anything!
- Accept any suggestions the children make and record some of their findings, for example, by:
   jotting down observations on sticky notes - stick them up on a blackboard or on planning sheets ready to talk about during a short 'plenary' session. taking photos and adding captions

Outdoor art gallery

What you want the children to learn or develop or develop

Show increasing independence in selecting and carrying out activities.

Linked areas of learning

Creative Development
Physical Development

Themed links

Senses, Colour, Days out

Resources

Boxes to use as display stands
Clothes line
Assorted papers

Paints, glue, sticky tape
Modelling clay
String for mobiles
Variety of collage materials including leaves, twigs, shells, feathers,
Washing-up bowl and towel

Ask the children if any of them have ever been to an art gallery. Talk about how we let people see any pictures or models that we like by putting them on display.

Take the children for a walk around your school, nursery or centre to look at items or features of interest and let them take photographs of things they liked.

Explain that they are going to help to set up a gallery in their outdoor area. Where should it be? Discuss the practicalities, for example not too close to the playing area. What will they put in their gallery? Paintings, models, sculpture, wall hangings, mobiles?

Encourage and expect each child to create something for the gallery by giving them easy access to a large variety of resources that will encourage their imagination.

Provide washing and drying facilities (a washing-up bowl and a towel). Have some prepared display stands (upturned boxes) and a wall/fence available where you can put up paintings.

■ Make a collection of materials available to create wall hangings and laminate them so that they can be hung up outside.

■ Extend the activity so that the gallery is included in role play with an entrance, exit signs, tickets, 'open' and 'closed' signs, and so on.

■ Adapt the idea to create an art gallery of natural, found materials – stones, shells, leaves, gravel.

What am I?

What you want the children to learn or develop
To work as part of a group in taking turns to play a game

Linked areas of learning
Communication, Language and Literacy
Physical Development

Themed links
Animals (but can be adapted for any topic)

Resources
Set of laminated cards with pictures (of animals, for example)
Velcro fastening or some way of attaching the card to clothing

This game is good for movement outside as well as encouraging social skills. The children quickly learn how to play the game for themselves, taking it in turns to be the guesser.

Prepare several sets of cards related to themes that would be good for outside activity, such as Transport, People who help us, Animals or Minibeasts.

Explain how to play. One child has a picture of an animal attached to their back. They do not know what it is. The other children can see what it is and, without using words, have to move like the animal so that the child can guess.

- Allow the children to sort themselves out as much as possible, but be prepared to act as mediator if necessary.
- Encourage them to follow the rules, for example taking turns, playing within a certain area.
- If the children want to, they can keep a tally.
- Encourage the children to give real clues by moving in the way the animal moves, for example.
- Take photos of the children for your records.

The dressing-up game

What you want the children to learn or develop
To dress and undress independently

Linked areas of learning
Problem Solving, Reasoning and Numeracy
Physical Development

Themed links
Counting, Clothes, Holidays or any role-play scenario

Resources
Large foam dice with numbers from one to six or pictures of items of clothing
Box of assorted clothing, for example hats, pairs of sunglasses (there must be the same number of items as children playing, in other words five hats for five children, and so on)
Board or prepared chart showing the number and corresponding item of clothing

This is a game that children need to be taught how to play and given time to learn. It is important that they are also encouraged to be flexible – not to be afraid to be inventive when playing, perhaps changing a rule if they want to.

It can, of course, be played inside, but outside there is space to throw a large foam dice and clothing could be hung on a washing line or hidden for children to find. Prepare a board with numbers one to six and a picture of an item of clothing by each number so that the children can see what to put on.

Children take turns to throw dice. The number they throw will correspond to an item of clothing that they then have to put on. The first person to be fully dressed is the winner. The clothing could be themed, for example winter clothes – hats, scarves, boots, coats or summer clothes – sunglasses, sun hats, T-shirts, sandals, and so on.

- Take time to teach the children how to play.
- When they are confident, be prepared to walk away and let them play by themselves.

Variation
- This game could be adapted for a sports day in the form of a team game – dress mum, dad or teacher!

Runaround rabbit

What you want the children to learn or develop
Show care and concern for others, for living things and the environment

Linked areas of learning
Communication, Language and Literacy
Creative Development

Themed links
Feelings, Senses, Myself, Families, Pets

Resources
A suitable toy for the outside area, for example an animal that would normally live outside like a rabbit, fox, badger, tortoise, hedgehog, bear
A basket/box

Introduce the rabbit (or other soft toy) and explain the scenario: each night the rabbit has the whole of the outdoor area to himself. When the children come in in the morning he has to share the area with them, but he's afraid so he hides. Where is he hiding today? He may be in a dark corner, on top of a wall or in the role-play area. He will need to have a basket or box where it is safe for him to stay during the day. Some children will like him to stay with them when they are playing outside.

- Hide the rabbit and be prepared to help the children look for him.
- Talk about where he might be.
- Play 'hot' and 'cold' – if the children are near the hiding place they are 'hot' and if not they are 'cold'
- Ask the children how they think rabbit feels if he is on top of a wall or in a dark place. Is he afraid? What will the children need to do to help rabbit feel better? A short discussion about how rabbit feels can often lead the children to explore emotions and perhaps talk about how they feel sometimes.
- Be mindful of positional language so that words such as 'in front of', 'beside' and 'next to' could be used.

Extension ideas
- Take photos of rabbit's hiding places to create a class book – good for positional language.
- Put up signs and directions to help children find the lost rabbit.

Stations

What you want the children to learn or develop
To consider the consequences of their actions (for themselves and others)

Linked areas of learning
Physical Development
Communication, Language and Literacy
Problem Solving, Reasoning and Numeracy

Themed links
Transport, Journeys

Resources
Four different-coloured cards, skittles or signs for the stations
Tape recorder and music

Divide an area so that there are four 'stations' or stopping points, and mark these areas with coloured cards, skittles or signs. The stations can be names, numbers, words or whatever is topical. Someone has control of the tape recorder and cannot see the stations and children - perhaps they have their back to the action.

The children run/walk around while the music is playing. When the music stops, the children must choose which station to stop at. The adult/child controlling the music then calls out a station and all of the children standing there are out of the game. The last person to stay in the game is the winner.

- Give the children time to make their choices.
- Encourage them to make their own decision and not always be with their friends.
- Be prepared to cope with children who are reluctant to be 'out'.
- Give children independence and let them play the game themselves.

Changing seats

What you want the children to learn or develop
To be able to play cooperative games

Linked areas of learning
Physical Development
Communication, Language and Literacy

Themed links
This game can be linked to any topic.

Resources
Somewhere the children can sit or stand in a circle
Carpet squares, logs, circles drawn with chalk

The object of the game is for the children to change places with each other. A caller says 'Change with someone else who has blue on/who has a pet rabbit/ who likes spaghetti, who has a letter 'e' in their name', and so on. It can be as easy or as difficult as you want and the children soon understand how to play. It is a fun game and can be played at a fast pace when the children understand what to do.

Teach the children how to play the game. Allow them plenty of time to think about what you've asked them, especially if they are young.

- Encourage them to change with different people and not always their best friend!
- Get them to play the game by themselves but be on hand to intervene when necessary.
- When they become experts, the questions can become more difficult, for example 'Change if you have a number two in your door number at home' or 'a letter 's' in your name'. The more able children will soon begin to think up questions for themselves.

Water Chain

What you want the children to learn or develop
To be able to work as part of a group

Linked areas of learning
Physical Development
Communication, Language and Literacy
Knowledge and Understanding of the World
Problem Solving, Reasoning and Numeracy

Themed links
Water, Journeys, Friends and neighbours

Resources
Chalk spots on the floor
Enough plastic jugs for each child to have one
Plastic aprons
Wellies for each child

This is a good game for children to encourage and teach each other. The object is for the water to be passed from one end of the line to the other. The children stand in a line on a spot. They each have a plastic jug.

You pour water into the first jug and the child has to pour it into their neighbour's, and so on. The child at the end pours it into a container again.

- Encourage the children to watch the water as they are pouring it and to try not to spill any.

- Encourage them to wait on their spot until it is their turn.
- It is possible to start with more water once the first amount has gone past three or four children so that the game can continue and the waits are not too long.
- Eventually, they can use a timer and see how long it will take them.

Blindfolded walk

What you want the children to learn or develop
To show care and concern for others
To become aware that there are some people who cannot see well

Linked areas of learning
Communication, Language and literacy
Physical Development

Themed links
Friends, Journeys

Resources
A long rope or several tied together, marking out a course on the floor (or a course set with masking tape)
A blindfold/scarf
Pairs of dark glasses

Set up a simple course with a long, thick rope on the floor, so the children have something to follow. Make sure the course is challenging - it might go around a tree, a shrub and up a slope.

The children will need to have a partner to work with. The object is for them to experience what it is like to move along without being able to see. They will need to wear a blindfold. Some children may not feel comfortable doing this and they should not be forced. Their partner will hold them and lead them around the track, telling them what is ahead.

Allow the children to experiment with this – obviously taking care that it is safe.
- Model the walk, showing them how to hold the arm

of their partner. Perhaps they can take an adult first? Maybe they will do it first with their eyes open and then use the blindfold afterwards.
- Talk to them about what it feels like. Were they scared?
- When the children are comfortable with this the walk can include climbing over, going under, and so on.

Wheelchair play

What you want the children to learn or develop
To experience and be aware that some people cannot walk and run well

To show care and concern for others

Linked areas of learning
Communication, Language and Literacy
Physical Development
Knowledge and Understanding of the World

Themed links
People who help us, Transport

Resources
A collection of walking sticks, crutches, wheelchairs (often the health centre, children's special needs services, St John's or Red Cross have old equipment they are willing to lend).

Talk to the children about how to use the equipment correctly. Allow for free play using the equipment provided.

Once they are familiar with it, set simple challenges, for example can they throw a ball into a bucket, or hit a target, while using the wheelchair? Can they steer around a course?

Start up conversations that will encourage children to talk. What does it feel like? What could they do to help other children who are in wheelchairs all the time or who have mobility problems?

Eventually the children will become aware of the difficulties some children are faced with.

Activities to support Communication Language and Literacy

We're going on a bear hunt

What you want the children to learn or develop
To interact with others and take account of what they say

Linked areas of learning
Problem Solving, Reasoning and Numeracy
Physical Development
Personal, Social and Emotional Development

Themed links
Teddy bears, Animals, Journeys, Story – We're Going on a Bear Hunt

Resources
We're Going on a Bear Hunt (Walker Books)
Teddy bear
Large cardboard box
Blanket
Strip of corrugated card
Soft, blue material (for river)
Art straws/long grasses

Read the story. Tell the children that they can re-enact the story outside using any of the equipment.

Provide a wide variety of resources but be prepared to respond if the children have other ideas for what they'd like to use. They may well use the equipment given but in a different way to that which you had planned.

Stand at a discrete distance and watch how they interact with each other. Be prepared to intervene sensitively if necessary.

- Encourage positional language when appropriate, for example going through a tunnel, over a bench, under a blanket. They can make a cave and hide the teddy inside.
- Encourage them to perform to friends/parents/the rest of the class.

- Suggest they make up an alternative ending, use another animal or have different obstacles.

If there is a piece of woodland or some trees nearby, some laminated signs or arrows and a bear cave can be so exciting! Signs could say:

'This way to the bear cave'
'Sssh! Bears asleep!',
'Please keep to the path',
'Danger!',
'To the woods'.

Letter hunt

What you want the children to learn or develop
To be able to recognise the letters in their own name

Linked areas of learning
Physical Development
Personal, Social and Emotional Development

Themed links
Explorers, Ourselves

Resources
Large, laminated name cards
Large, single alphabet letters
Large timer

Put the letters all around the outdoor area so that they can be easily seen. Hang them over a wooden fence, on hooks along a wall or scatter them on the grass.

The children you want to target should each have their name card and can run around looking for their letters in the order in which they appear on their cards. They will collect them up and could perhaps place them under or over their name cards. As they get used to the game, they

can leave their cards in a central place and find their letters by remembering the letter shape they want next.

Give the children time to do this, helping them at first. Some children especially like playing the game against a timer. How quickly can they find their letters? Has the timer run out?

Extension ideas
- The game can be extended to include looking for significant words – perhaps linked to the theme.
- Older children enjoy finding words and rearranging them into a sentence that may relate to a story/theme.

Writing in mud/sand

What you want the children to learn or develop
To use writing as a means of recording and communicating

Linked areas of learning
Knowledge and Understanding of the World
Problem Solving, Reasoning and Numeracy

Themed links
Shapes, Materials, Earth, Counting, Transport

Resources
Large shallow tray
Damp earth/mud/sand
Variety of writing implements, for example sticks, twigs, feathers
An activity for the child to record

This activity is used widely as an open-ended play activity but it can also be used in a more focused way. Prepare a large tray – builders' trays are wonderful for this – and fill it with wet sand/mud. Provide a wide variety of writing implements such as twigs and feathers of different thicknesses and sizes.

Decide which child will be the writer and agree on an activity. This can be how many times a child can complete a course on their bike without knocking something over, or how many times they can throw a bean bag into a box – simple activities that can easily be counted.

Be prepared to allow the children time to experiment with how they want to record and be open to their suggestions.

At first the children might want to use tally marks.

It is important to encourage the child to count up the marks and relate it to the game – 'Meg was able to catch three balls wasn't she? Let's check!' In this way, the children will begin to see that the marks mean something.

Extension idea
- The children can use blackboards, flipcharts, paper and clipboards and chalks on the floor.

Dig for letters

What you want the children to learn or develop
To consolidate the learning/awareness of letter sounds and shapes that may be a focus of the week

Linked areas of learning
Knowledge and Understanding of the World

Themed links
Treasure, Ourselves, Underground
Resources
Sets of plastic letter shapes
Bulb fibre, earth or sand
Large lightweight plastic flower tubs or pots
Small trowels

This activity is a great favourite as children of all ages love playing hide and seek. Fill the large pots (boxes, builders' tray, sand pit or grow-bags) with earth, bulb fibre or sand and bury a set number of letters. Encourage the children to look for the letters and, once found, match them against their name or prepared laminated cards.

Model the activity. Be patient and allow them time to really search. Stand back and only intervene when invited or it seems necessary.

Refer to the letters found so that the links are made with the indoor learning, for example, 'Do you remember that was the letter we looked at in our game?'

- Try using a timer – some children like being set a challenge!
- As they become used to the activity the children can organise themselves and play it with partners – one hiding the letters and the other finding them.
- Younger children will enjoy just looking for the letters and perhaps finding another the same.
- Older or more able children can find letters that make a word – perhaps making the word on a magnetic board.

Magic carpet journey

What you want the children to learn or develop
To use talk in imaginary situations

Linked areas of learning
Knowledge and Understanding of the World
Creative Development

Themed links
Journeys, Fairy stories
Resources
Carpet/blanket
Maps/atlas/globe
Treasure box
Photo album
Costumes and artefacts from a variety of cultures
Magic wand, genie lamp
Egg timer/alarm clock
Suitcases
Notebooks

Prepare a resource box containing magical, exciting props and set it up outside. Take the children for a ride on the magic carpet, modelling the play and telling a story. Encourage the children to contribute to the story and be prepared to include their characters and plots.

Introduce a puppet character who loves to go on adventures. Take lots of photos of the puppet character in different settings to help the children, for example on the beach, in the forest, at the airport, at the park, in another country.

Talk with the children about their feelings on the journey and ask open-ended questions about what they think they might see when they get there.

- More able children will enjoy talking into a dictaphone.
- Tickets for the journey can be prepared and sold
- Time schedules can be planned in advance and signs made announcing departures, and so on.

Variation
- This is a really good activity at Christmas time when the children can take the magic carpet to Lapland. Provide white sheets for snow, thick blankets, warm gloves, hot water bottles and cups of cocoa!

Message in a bottle

What you want the children to learn or develop
To be able to make marks as a means of communicating with someone else

Linked areas of learning:
Knowledge and Understanding of the World
Physical Development

Themed links
Water, Islands
Resources
An assortment of paper
A container with water – water tray, baby bath, drain pipes or water channels
A hose pipe
A variety of bottles – plastic and glass
An assortment of writing implements - chalk, charcoal, pencils, old feathers (quills), twigs

This is the type of play that appeals to all children and especially those that are active and physical - even they will love 'writing'! The idea is for the children to experiment with writing messages, placing them in a bottle and sending them to someone else to read. The desert island scenario is the obvious choice for this and the role-play area can be set up around the water area. The children will thoroughly enjoy making a water channel in which to post their message. Use drain pipes, hoses and plastic boxes (to catch the water) or just have the water tray out. Obviously if glass bottles are used great care must be taken but it would be a great pity if the children couldn't use the real thing.

Take part in the play – encourage the children to make up a story about being on an island. Discuss what they can do to get help – what could they do?

- Show them how to write a message, place it inside a bottle and send it across the water.
- Encourage them to experiment with writing using all types of implements – dipping twigs in mud is huge fun!
- Which bottles float best? Does the water get in and spoil the message?

Letters

What you want the children to learn or develop
To be able to recognise the letters of the alphabet

Linked areas of learning:
Problem Solving, Reasoning and Numeracy
Physical Development

Themed links
This game can be played at any time and linked to any topic.

Resources
Masking tape
Laminated cards of letters
Large letter shapes for the children to hold

This is a simple game that can be changed to suit and can include as few or as many letters/numbers as required. It can be played to consolidate learning that may have been introduced inside - perhaps the children have been learning about two letters and they are familiar with three others. It is fun to play and is one way of making literacy more appealing to children who prefer to be active.

Decide on the letters for the week and use the masking tape to mark areas/stations on the tarmac outside. The stations should each have a letter attached to them and the children given letters to hold. The children run/walk/skip around the areas until you hold up a letter shape. The children holding the matching letter run to the area that matches their shape. The other children stand still.

Make sure that all of the children have a go at running to their area and change the letter shapes they are holding on a regular basis – keep it flowing.

Once they know how to play this game, the children can take charge of it themselves - you will find that they soon organise themselves very well. This provides an ideal opportunity for you to assess the children.

This type of game can be left outside and played for a few minutes each day. It is surprising how quickly some children will learn their letter sounds and shapes by holding the letters, looking to match, and moving. It makes it fun and you may find that some who do not respond indoors will be keen to join in outdoors!

In the pond

What you want the children to learn or develop
To be able to listen attentively and follow simple instructions

Linked areas of learning
Physical Development
Problem Solving, Reasoning and Numeracy

Themed links
Water, Life cycles (tadpoles/frogs)
A game to play at any time

Resources
A long rope
Chalk
Masking tape

This game is huge fun to play with whole groups or small numbers. It involves children being 'out' so opportunities arise for coping with this – some children find it difficult!

Place a rope on a flat area. This is the pond. The children all stand around the edge of the pond, on the bank. The caller will say 'In the pond' and the children have to jump over the rope into the pond. Then maybe 'On the bank' is called and the children jump on to the bank. So far so good! The caller then tries to catch the children out by calling 'On the pond' or 'In the bank' and the children are to stay where they are. If they jump, they are out!

- Explain carefully to the children what they have to do.
- Begin the game slowly to make sure the children understand how to play.
- Get some other adults to join in and demonstrate the game.
- Once they are familiar with the rules the children can be callers.
- Emphasise the words on and in.
- Later, cards could be held up instead of calling out.

There are many simple games such as this that are excellent for developing listening skills and if they are used on a frequent basis the children will soon become experts!

Letter from a lost teddy

What you want the children to learn or develop
To know that print carries meaning

Linked areas of learning

Problem Solving, Reasoning and Numeracy
Physical Development
Knowledge and Understanding of the World

Themed links

Any story or topic of the time!

Resources

A large print letter written from teddy, a giant or other character
A variety of objects for the children to find
Some messages

Decide what characters you want to introduce. It might be that a letter arrives from a story character, such as the wolf from 'The Three Little Pigs', the giant from 'Jack and the Beanstalk', the hungry caterpillar or the teddy who had a picnic.

The letter could ask the children to look for lost items, such as food for a picnic or characters, such as the three pigs. You might want to include a map showing where the items are. The children then have to see if they can find them. You could place messages by the hidden items saying 'Dig here' or 'Look up'.

Base the letter on an interesting scenario that the children are involved with – it could even be a dinosaur that has lost its eggs!

- Be ready to interpret the messages and enable them to follow the instructions.
- Be ready to pose questions and hypothesise: 'Do you think ….?', 'What could be here?'
- Once the children understand the hunt they might like to reply to the character saying what they found and where. The character can then reply.

Kim's game with a difference!

What you want the children to learn or develop

To be able to talk, anticipate, ask questions and make close observations

Linked areas of learning

Problem Solving, Reasoning and Numeracy
Creative Development
Physical Development

Themed links

Opposites

Resources

Something for one group of children to go into, for example a tent, a large box, a role-play house
A large sheet/blanket or tarpaulin

You will need to supervise this game but it is great fun and all children love it! Two groups of children are needed. One group to be 'seen' and memorised, the other to go into the tent and wait for a few moments. A member of the first group then hides and the rest of the group lie on the ground and are covered with the blanket or sheet. The second group come out, take off the sheet and see if they know who is hiding.

- Encourage the children to take ownership of the game. Let them decide who is going to hide first.
- Decide if there should be rules - Who will guess? How will they guess?
- Instead of removing a child from the scene, they take off a cardigan, a watch, a hairband, and so on. The second group will really need to observe carefully. If they do not spot the difference immediately they may ask questions.

The rope walk

What you want the children to learn or develop
To count reliably up to ten

Linked areas of learning
Physical Development
Communication, Language and Literacy
Knowledge and Understanding of the World

Themed links
Journeys, Stories, Colour, Animals

Resources
Long rope
Assortment of everyday objects, for example feather, shell, pebble or small toys – a dog, cat, rabbit

Place a long wiggly rope around the outside area, preferably on grass, around shrubs and trees. (It is much more exciting if the children can't see where the rope ends.) Place ten objects along the rope, on either side, at a reasonable distance. They could be in the grass or under the shrubs but still able to be seen.

The children walk slowly along the rope pathway looking for the objects but they must not pick them up! They can count them as they walk along but are not to tell anyone else about them.

Once they reach the end of the rope they can whisper to an adult how many objects they could see. They might be able to recall what the objects were. Be prepared to allow the children plenty of time. Some will want to go back again and again.

Variations
- The activity can be adapted in many ways, for example 'How many blue things could you find?' 'Did you see three? Go back and see if you can spot two more!' 'What animals did you see?' 'What story do you think the objects are from?'
- A plan can be drawn and the children can place the objects according to the plan.
- The children can work in pairs.

Stepping stones

What you want the children to learn or develop
To say with confidence the number that is one more than a given number

Linked areas of learning
Communication, Language and Literacy
Physical Development

Themed links
Rivers, Journeys, Stories
Resources
Ten log slices, painted with numbers
Two ropes

Log slices are fairly light but cumbersome and need to be manoeuvred by the children. This is good for the arm muscles which need to be strong for developing the fine motor skills needed for writing later on.

They can be bought quite cheaply at most logging yards. Choose slices that are flat and paint numbers on them. The children can play with them and put them in order.

Introduce the story of 'The Billy Goats Gruff' and see if they can make a bridge for the goats to cross, using the ropes as riverbanks.

Encourage the children to shout out the numbers as they step on each one and then extend it so they are calling out the number that comes after.

- Ask the child to stop on the stepping stone that comes after three and to call out the number.
- Use vocabulary such as 'one more than'.
- Encourage the child who is unsure to have a go.
- Allow the children to be inventive when playing.

The old woman who lived in a shoe

What you want the children to learn or develop
One-to-one correspondence of numbers to nine

Linked areas of learning
Communication, Language and Literacy
Physical Development

Themed links
Nursery rhymes, Clothes, Homes

Resources
A large cut-out shoe – plastic, cardboard or drawn with chalk
Mob hat for the old woman to wear (or hat for boys to be an old man)

This game is best played with a small group of children – up to nine. The children pretend to play outside the shoe and one of the children is the old woman (or man) inside. The old woman calls to her children to come in. She may call two girls and four boys or three girls and one boy, according to who is playing in the game. She may post a notice saying 'Three boys please!'. They have to look and keep checking that the right number has gone in.

The rules of the game are very fluid; it is all about calling out the number and checking constantly that the right number is in the shoe. The old woman is the 'counter',

providing the opportunity to consolidate counting skills whilst enjoying the game. Sometimes the children need to be in an orderly queue to be counted!

Extension ideas
- To extend the game, give each child a number and the old woman calls out the numbers that she wants inside.
- To extend it even further, she calls out a total and the children with cards that add to the total must step inside.

The hungry caterpillar

What you want the children to learn or develop
To use appropriate shapes (with their bodies) to make representational models

Linked areas of learning
Communication, Language and Literacy
Knowledge and Understanding of the World
Physical Development

Themed links
Fruit, Food, Minibeasts, Life cycles

Resources
A large mat, hoop or rope that could represent the fruit basket or a basket shape drawn on the floor with chalks
Laminated pictures of pieces of fruit

Read The Hungry Caterpillar by Eric Carle (Puffin) to the children. They may already be familiar with the story, but this time they need to think about the shapes of the fruit in the story and how they can make that shape with their body, for example a long, thin shape for the banana, a round shape for the apple.

Talk about the fruit in the story and how they could turn the story into a game. Encourage one child to be the caterpillar and the others (up to six) to be the fruit. The children run around the 'basket' until the caterpillar calls out which fruit goes in the basket, for example 'Two oranges', 'One apple' or all the bananas! The children go to the basket making the appropriate shape.

Encourage the children to make up their own games about the story and be prepared to try their ideas.

It is important to link their body shape with the fruit so that they begin to try to make representations.

- Refer to children that are trying hard and are successful.
- Always be flexible but still challenging those that are more able. Can they arrange the rest of the children in the order of the fruit in the story? How many cherries do they need?

The circle game

What you want the children to learn or develop
To be able to talk about and recreate simple patterns

Linked areas of learning
Communication, Language and Literacy
Personal, Social and Emotional Development

Themed links
Shapes, Patterns

Resources
No specific resources required

The children make a circle outside; up to 12 children is probably best. They are going to make a sequential pattern with their bodies so you will need to show them what to do first. For example:

One child whispers name – next child shouts – next whispers
One child claps hands – next waves – next claps
One child touches floor – next tries to touch the sky
One child places hands on head – next hands on feet
Each time refer to the pattern and allow them plenty of time to work out for themselves what they need to do.

Younger children will enjoy the simple ideas but the older ones can make quite complicated patterns, maybe using sequences of three or four.

They may want to try to predict what their movement will be or represent their movement on paper.

The children themselves can lead the movements and some will really enjoy thinking up some interesting movements for the others to copy!

Refer to any pattern making or sequence work they might have been doing inside, for example block printing or playing with bricks and show them the links to doing it with their bodies outside.

Treasure hunt

What you want the children to learn or develop
To count reliably up to ten objects
To recognise numerals

Linked areas of learning
Communication, Language, Literacy
Knowledge and Understanding of the World
Physical Development

Themed links
Treasure, Journeys, Underground
The children are always keen to hunt for things – treasure is a favourite!

Resources
Laminated photos of areas or objects in the outdoor area, such as tree, bench, sandpit
Gold/silver nuggets/treasure
Number cards
Clipboards and resources for recording

Take photographs of places in the outside area and laminate them. They can be used over and over again for many games. Hang the pictures on a fence, on hooks or put them on an outside task board.

The object for this game is for the children to find the area from the photo and look for treasure that will be buried or hidden near there, for example in a tub, under a flower pot, in the earth (marked by a cross!) Be inventive! Once they have found the treasure, they count how many pieces and place a number card by the side.

- Make sure the treasure is not too easily found - they need to hunt!
- Allow time for the children to really enjoy the game but make sure once they have completed a 'find' that it is checked.
- Perhaps they can be encouraged to devise a system for recording what treasure and how many pieces they found by each photo – using a clipboard or a large board, writing in a builders' tray full of mud?
- Be mindful of the skills you want the children to learn. This time it is to encourage accurate counting – much better to count treasure than small counters!

Variation
- Let the children bury the treasure for you to find sometimes - or for a partner.

Humpty Dumpty

What you want the children to learn or develop
To use everyday words to describe the position of Humpty (on top, behind, next to, near, beside)

Linked areas of learning
Communication, Language and Literacy
Physical Development
Knowledge and Understanding of the World

Themed links
Buildings, Nursery rhymes

Resources
A collection of house bricks (DIY stores sell small bricks at 20p each)
Humpty Dumpty toy/puppet

Most children will be familiar with the nursery rhyme 'Humpty Dumpty' and will enjoy re-enacting the story. The idea is for children to use the bricks to build a wall for Humpty. This is particularly good for developing upper arm muscles. You may need to lead the game at first and ask the children where to put Humpty.

Talk to the children about how to carry and move the bricks safely. (The walls shouldn't be too high or they could topple and hurt someone.)

Talk to them about the patterns made when building a wall and how to build it so that it is stable.

Discuss where to put Humpty. Use the position words such as 'on top of', 'behind', 'in front of', 'beside', 'next to', and use another toy to extend this activity, for example a mouse, a smaller egg.

- Older children can draw a plan and put Humpty on it for their partner to place accurately.
- Younger children might like to make small, individual walls and place hard-boiled eggs on them.
- Make a story that involves the children placing Humpty on/off/beside the wall, and so on.

Shape mobiles

What you want the children to learn or develop
To become aware of the shape of a triangle

Linked areas of learning
Creative Development
Physical Development
Communication, Language and Literacy

Themed links
Shapes, Weather, Wood, Three

Resources
Twigs in assorted sizes
String
Strands of wool
Feathers, ribbons, leaves, small twigs, long grasses

The children make a frame using three twigs joined with string. They string wool in the space between and can then thread a variety of items through the wool.

Model how to make the frame and encourage them to fasten it themselves using the string. It can be frustrating so be prepared to step in and help when needed.

Encourage the children to decorate their frame using natural found materials.

- Talk with the children about the number of twigs they used and what shapes they have made.
- Be aware of the learning objective but be led by the children's own interest in what they are doing.
- Use the correct vocabulary – 'shape', 'sides', 'triangle', 'angles' (if appropriate).
- Hang the frames from trees or fences or make a temporary display area with a washing line.
- Encourage a group of children to make a collaborative triangle, a large one that can be on permanent display.

The great cereal box line

What you want the children to learn or develop
To be able to order items by length
To talk about longer and shorter

Linked areas of learning
Communication, Language and Literacy
Physical Development
Creative Development

Themed links
Lines, Measurement, Buildings

Resources
An assortment of cereal boxes, as many as possible, stuffed and sealed so that they are solid and strong

Challenge the children to see if they can reach a point by making a line with the boxes. They will need to place them one after the other.

Make sure there are lots of boxes to choose from. Set a realistic challenge. Encourage the children to guess how many boxes it will take.

Make up a game using the boxes. Perhaps use a timer. The boxes could be at one end of the area and the children have to run to collect them one at a time.

- Could two groups of children play a game against each other? Who can make the line first?
- How long can the line get? Can it be made so that it goes all around the area?
- The boxes can be used as building bricks. How many can the children put one on top of the other without them falling over?
- Encourage talk about length - long, short, more, longer, bigger, smaller.

Skittles

What you want the children to learn or develop
To be able to recognise number shapes and say the name

Linked areas of learning
Communication, Language and Literacy
Physical Development
Personal, Social and Emotional Development

Themed links
Numbers A game to play at any time

Resources
Plastic water bottles – small and large
Sand, water, earth, gravel or anything that will stabilise the bottles
Numbers painted on the bottles
A large ball and a smaller ball

The children will enjoy collecting the bottles and then deciding what to use to fill them. Provide a variety of fillings and set the challenge of finding out which is the best for keeping the bottles upright.

Give the children time to experiment with the fillings. Let them fill and empty until they are satisfied with the results.

Decide how many skittles to use for the game. Put numbers on the sides of the bottles - ten large bottles and ten small. Use the large bottles to play a game of skittles with a large ball. Ask the children to try and knock over number four, for example. Or they can start with number one and try to knock them over in order.

Substitute the large bottles with small ones to make it more challenging.

The game can be adapted for all children and is much more meaningful to them if they have made their own.

Activities to support Knowledge and Understanding of the World

Bug/minibeast hunt

What you want the children to learn or develop
To identify some features of living things

Linked areas of learning
Problem Solving, Reasoning and Numeracy
Communication, Language and Literacy
Personal, Social and Emotional Development

Themed links
Growth, Minibeasts, Big and little (Opposites), Animal homes

Resources
Variety of collecting containers
Magnifying lenses
Plastic gloves for those who would like them
Identification books
Labels
Log pile
Collection of flower pots, rocks and bricks

Arrange the log pile or put the old bricks, flower pots and rocks in a shady corner of the outdoor area so that minibeasts will be encouraged to the habitat.

Talk to the children about being careful with the insects they find and to put them back where they found them. Let the children go hunting for creatures and show them how to capture them safely.

Encourage them to really look at their minibeasts and compare them to others found.

Younger children will be happy collecting and identifying whilst older children can be asked to find specific creatures, for example you could prepare a set of laminated pictures and ask the children to look for only those. Hang them on a wall with hooks. Discuss where they were found. How many different types can they find over by the wall? Under the flower pots?

Prepare a chart/map so that the capable children can record where they find the minibeasts.

Photos hide and seek

What you want the children to learn or develop
To notice features of their environment and talk about them

Linked areas of learning
Communication, Language and Literacy
Problem Solving, Reasoning and Numeracy

Themed links
Materials, Journeys, Senses
Resources
Photographs of up to 20 features of the outdoor area
Hooks, clips or some means of easily attaching the photo to its feature
Number cards and recording equipment

Prepare as many photographs of the outdoor area as you can and laminate them so that they can be out in all weathers. Make some of them quite difficult, for example the side of the bench, a part of the flower tub. They can be used in all sorts of games and the children will be very inventive if given the chance.

Give the children a photo and let them see if they can match it up with the original object or feature. There may be two or three photos of the same item, taken from different angles. They should be able to fix the photo on or next to the feature.

Talk with the children about how they found the items. What was noticeable?

Give each feature a number and leave the photos in a central area. The children have to take the number to the photo to match it or draw the number by the photo.

Extension ideas

- Let the children use a digital camera to take their own shots and produce their own trail.
- As they become used to this type of observation, make the photos more detailed - just take a small part of a feature.
- Play a memory game – what did you see first? Then what?

Eeyore's house

What you want the children to learn or develop
To build with a purpose

Linked areas of learning
Problem Solving, Reasoning and Numeracy
Physical Development
Creative Development

Themed links
Houses and homes, Buildings/shelters, Winnie the Pooh stories, Measuring

Resources
The story of Eeyore from 'Winnie the Pooh'
A range of sizes of twigs and sticks, preferably scattered around the outside area
An Eeyore soft toy (or any donkey)
Some pieces of rope or string in different lengths

Read the story of 'Winnie the Pooh'. Eeyore doesn't have a house and Pooh Bear decides to build one for him. Encourage the children to find the sticks and twigs and build a house for Eeyore. You can go for a walk to the park or local woodland to collect twigs. Ask children to see if they can find some as long as their arms, some as small as their hands, some that will go up to their elbows. Suggest ways in which the twigs can be tied together but let the children try their own methods, too. Have an Eeyore toy ready so the children can try out their house.

- Be ready to intervene if a child is finding their idea difficult to carry out.

- Allow them time to revisit their constructions to improve or refine them.
- Extend the idea so that some children might make a larger construction, or one for something else.
- If possible, collect some large branches and put a frame against a tree/fence/wall so that a den can be built and the children can use it for a huge variety of imaginative play.

Weather watch

What you want the children to learn or develop
To start developing first-hand investigational skills

Linked areas of learning
Communication, Language and Literacy
Problem Solving, Reasoning and Numeracy

Themed links
Weather, Change, Growth, Patterns

Resources
Shallow trays
Plastic containers to collect rain
Wind socks
Ribbons/streamers on sticks
Kites
Windmills
Chalks
Plastic guttering
Plastic sheets
Sunglasses
Wellingtons
Umbrellas
Weather chart

Ask the children 'What is the weather today?' and start a discussion about the types of weather we have. What clothes are the children wearing? Did they wear a coat to nursery/school? Predict what the weather might be like tomorrow – use a weather chart (put one outside on a chalkboard).

Collect rainfall (or snow) in a plastic container over a week or longer. Record which day had the most rain (or snow). Look at puddles to see where they form and how long they stay on the ground. Collect and watch rain in drainpipes. Give the children the resources to make their own water course – pipes, buckets of water, hoses.

Set the children a task of designing and making a way of collecting water, using some polythene sheeting. Leave a saucer, or shallow container with water, outside on a very cold day or a hot day to see what happens.

Make and test wind socks and windmills. Which direction is the wind blowing? Fly kites.

If it is foggy, how far can the children see at certain times of the day? On sunny days, where are the shadows?

- Encourage the children to talk about what they are doing.
- Engage them in conversation that will include decision-making, for example 'Shall I hang the washing out now? Will it dry?' Ask them to describe whether they can feel the wind, sun or cold.
- Have a supply of weather songs, rhymes and poems available.
- Encourage the children to set up a role play that will have weather as a focus, for example a beach café, a shop that sells kites, a washing line for hanging out the clothes.

- Set up a weather forecast studio outside/inside.
- Make suggestions at times when the musical instruments can be used to enhance the play, for example a triangle for rain, cymbals for thunder.

Build a nest

What you want the children to learn or develop
To be able to construct with a purpose

Linked areas of learning
Physical Development
Creative Development

Themed links
Birds, Flight, Homes, Spring

Resources
Small flexible twigs such as willow
Mosses
Leaves
Feathers
Long grasses
Any suitable soft material

The children may have been reading stories about birds or finding out about their habits and life cycle. There are many story books that may be good starting points for this activity but the best thing is to find a real nest and examine how it was built, showing the children how clever the bird was to interweave all of the different fibres and textures.

Explain to the children that they could build a nest for a bird. You may be able to supply a toy, puppet or model for the nests. Encourage them to find some twigs that are all about the size of their lower arms/hands and try to weave them into a round shape. (Some children may need help and could work in pairs.) They then need some soft materials to line the nests – have plenty available strewn around the outdoor area so that the children have to look for it rather than have it provided for them!

● Encourage them to talk about the soft material, how it feels to touch, and about having to make the nest strong on the outside.
● If you have trees/shrubs in the outdoor area, put the nests in them and test how strong they are in bad weather.
● Children really enjoy this activity and will build the nests time and time again. If so, extend it and make a collection of as many types of nests as you can but also find pictures and information about other creatures that nest.

Snapshot

What you want the children to learn or develop
To be able to identify some features of living things

Linked areas of learning
Communication, Language and Literacy
Problem Solving, Reasoning and Numeracy

Themed links
Seasons, Minibeasts

Resources
Hoops/ropes (something to define an area of grass/earth)
Magnifying glasses
Collecting boxes

Paper and pencils
Spades

The children will need to decide which part of the garden, grass or soil to work on, and put their hoop or rope down. Ask them to focus on the area inside their hoop and to look carefully to see what is inside.

Encourage the children to say what they can see in their space. How many dandelions can they count? Can they spot any moving creatures? What are they?

You might encourage the children to draw a sketch of the things they have in their area or make a more detailed observational drawing of a specific item. Have plenty of paper available for drawing.

Some children will say they can't see anything! Let them dig into a small part of the area to see what is underneath the surface.

● Have magnifying glasses and collecting boxes available for those that would like to study their finds further.
● Talk to the children about the habitat and explain how important it is that we leave the creatures and flowers there to flourish.
● Go back the following week to see if the area has changed and again throughout the year as the seasons change.

Make a bridge

What you want the children to learn or develop
To be confident to try out a range of tools and techniques safely

Linked areas of learning
Creative Development
Physical Development
Problem Solving, Reasoning and Numeracy
Communication, Language and Literacy

Themed links

Bridges, Transport, Islands, Rivers, Water

Resources

Planks, tyres, bricks, plastic crates, tarpaulins
Clothes pegs
Ropes
Masking tape

The children make a bridge that will carry them from one area to another.

First, you need to set the scene. Make up a story that involves the children being stranded on an island. They need to cross a river/chasm to survive. Mark out the area they need to cross to make it as realistic as possible.

Provide lots of large equipment for them to experiment with.

Only intervene if absolutely necessary and allow the children to fail sometimes. They will learn through failure as long as it is done in a positive caring way.

Once completed, celebrate their achievement and maybe retell the story or encourage the children to make one up of their own.

- Encourage the children to tell others how they have made their bridge and if possible to give reasons why they chose to do it in that way.
- Encourage them to make other types of bridges, small and large, and find pictures of some famous ones, for example the Severn Bridge, the Forth Bridge, The Golden Gate.

Make a go-kart

What you want the children to learn or develop

That pushes and pulls make things move and are types of force

Linked areas of learning

Physical Development
Creative Development
Problem Solving, Reasoning and Numeracy

Themed links

Transport, Wheels, Journeys, Islands

Resources

Large boxes
Wheels
Ropes
Planks of wood
Dowling
Broom handles

The children make a kart to take them along.

Set the scene – give them a scenario or put the activity into a context. For example, tell them a story about being stranded and someone hurting their ankle and needing transport. It is always so much more exciting if the children have a reason for building.

Provide them with the equipment or show them where they can make their choices. The equipment must be as real as possible so safety talks are essential.

Be near to hand so that when a child needs help to move their idea on it can be provided if at all possible.

- Encourage the children to hypothesise and have a go and let them fail if necessary. This is a really good learning experience if carried out in a supportive way.
- Talk with them about how best to join their pieces of equipment so that they do not fall off and listen to all of their ideas.
- Encourage them to show others and celebrate their inventions.
- Talk with them about why it is difficult to move something along and try pushing and pulling along different surfaces.

- Some children may want to make their own small versions of go-karts to carry soft toys.

Leaf threading

What you want the children to learn or develop
To be aware of similarities and difference

Linked areas of learning
Physical Development
Creative Development
Problem Solving, Reasoning and Numeracy

Themed links
Weather, Trees, Wood (Materials)

Resources
Lots of leaves, preferably lying on the ground
An assortment of twigs of differing lengths

The children need to choose a length of twig that is about the length of their forearm. They can have fun measuring. They then collect leaves to thread onto the twigs.

Discuss with the children how to handle the twigs, for example not to lift them high and to carry them down by the side of their bodies. Look at the leaves and talk with the children about the colours, patterns and sizes. Encourage them to collect leaves that are similar in some way whether it is size, shape or colour.

- Ask them to collect five leaves and show them how to thread them onto the twigs.
- Encourage them to collect five more.
- How many can they thread onto their twig?
- Hang the twigs up outside and watch them dance in the wind.

Planting bulbs

What you want the children to learn or develop
To understand that bulbs need to be planted in order to grow

Linked areas of learning
Physical Development

Themed links
Growing, Under the ground, Water, Seasons
Resources
A grow-bag
Some bulbs
A trowel

Put the grow-bag outside where the children can easily use it – perhaps on a low wall or small table or on the floor.

Talk with the children about bulbs. Show them how they peel and are made of many layers. Show them the top and bottom. It is important that the children have a chance to handle the bulbs and play with them before planting seriously.

Encourage them to plant them in the grow-bag. Let them experiment with the planting – digging them up – and planting again. When they are ready, they can plant some bulbs into a pot themselves. Encourage them to write their name on a label and water the bulbs regularly.

Activities to support Physical Development

Promoting thinking skills outdoors

The very fact that the children are outside and have the freedom to engage in large-scale play is supporting their physical development, particularly in strengthening their muscles and developing large motor skills.

You need to provide a range of exciting resources that will immediately stimulate the children's imagination so that they will want to carry that plank and join it to the plastic crate to make a runway, for example. Carrying and managing unwieldy items can be challenging for children and of course there is always the safety aspect of allowing children to use 'adult' resources but lightweight plastic building bricks do not build muscles!

Almost every activity suggested for the other five areas of learning has some physical aspect to it. Here are some examples of combining physical development with promoting thinking skills.

You need to start with a basic collection of resources.

Basic resources for promoting thinking skills outdoors
Cardboard boxes in assorted sizes
Corrugated card
Assorted lengths of plastic pipes (guttering, drain pipes)
Assorted lengths of planks of wood
Dowling, cut into lengths the same size
Clear plastic tubing, lengths of flexible tubing
Ropes, twine
Plastic crates
Assorted sizes of wheels
Tarpaulin, blankets, heavy duty plastic sheeting
Clothes horse
Enough building bricks to build
Flower pots, buckets, plastic bottles of all sizes
Hoops, hooks, pulleys

Wallpaper table (with legs cut down to an appropriate height for young children)
Masking tape

Supply a range of meaningful, exciting resources that will immediately stimulate conversation (see list of basic resources).

Take time to look through it with the children, using open-ended questions wherever possible to encourage their imagination, for example 'I wonder what this flexible tubing could be used for when we build our fire engine?' Be ready to accept their suggestions.

- Be ready to plant the seed of an idea rather than dictate an outcome.
- Give the children challenges.
- Always have a time for evaluation when you can talk about what the children were doing. This is the time to encourage refinement, if appropriate.
- Take lots of photographs.

Desert island scenario

The children are left on a desert island and need to attract the attention of a passing small aircraft/ helicopter (see also page 51).

- Put some stakes in the ground with a rope tied to one of them. Can the children make a shape for the helicopter to see from the sky? A letter 'H' for help?
- Using this activity set the challenge of how many letters of the alphabet they can make, or 2-D shapes?
- It is beginning to get dark and the weather isn't good – they need a shelter.
- Supply the children with the resources and ask them to build a shelter for themselves or two people. Is it waterproof? Will it blow away if it becomes windy? What could they do to make it even better? Some

children will enjoy making small dens/homes for toys or the class puppet.

- The children need to get a message to someone so they can be rescued. What could they use?
- Supply them with a bucket/s of water, water tray, or container that will hold water. Let them experiment with messages in bottles (see page 33). What will they need to write? Will the message get wet?
- Use balloons to extend this activity. Make parachutes with messages attached and launch them!
- There is a wet and boggy area that the children need to cross. Can they do this using the equipment provided? What else do they need?
- Use planks, tyres, bricks and crates to make a bridge.
- Make it realistic by giving them an area to cross – use ropes to create the edges of the area, chalk lines or masking tape.
- There is a long beach area on the island and the children could be challenged to make a vehicle.
- Provide the children with large cardboard boxes, wheels, ropes and planks of wood. Be prepared to help follow their ideas and provide them with the equipment they think they may need (within reason!)
- It is important that they try out their ideas. Give them the chance to explain what they are trying to do.

- The children need to collect water for drinking. What can they use?
- Let the children experiment with drainpipes and guttering, tubes, funnels and buckets. Place some guttering on a slope attached to a wall with brackets. Watch the water run down.
- See how much water can be collected in a week. How and where can it be recorded?

An outdoor curriculum based around Where the Wild Things are by Maurice Sendak

Scenario 1

Max is angry and cross. He is trying to make a den and pretending to be a wolf.

- What do you need to make a den?
- How would you make it?
- What would it need to have for shelter?

Provide rope, blankets, clothes horse, pegs, cardboard boxes.

Study pictures of wolves – What type of ears/nose do they have? Make a collection of materials to make wolf masks. How can we make a wolf mask? What materials shall we use? How could you make his long bushy tail? Provide card, cloth, scissors, fur - a collection for children to choose from, books and pictures from the internet.

Scenario 2

Max went to bed and that night a forest grew.

- What must we have for a forest?
- What can we do to make a forest?
- What plants are found in a forest?

Provide containers and pots, bulb fibre, earth, canes, seeds, slices of tree trunk, sticks and branches, leaves, paper, material, artificial flowers.

Look in books for pictures of jungles and forests. Choose the best place for Foley Forest.

Scenario 3

Max found an ocean and a boat and he sailed away.

- What is an ocean? What does it smell of?
- How can we make a boat? What do we need?

Provide water in the water tray and some small boats to explore with, plastic crates, drainpipes, guttering, ropes, large sheets, planks, buckets, boxes.

Make a collection of things that are found in the ocean – shells, pebbles, fish (real or pictures). Have a sensory area with salt, pebbles, sand and water either inside or out or both.

Scenario 4

Max sailed to a land where the wild things are.

- What did they look like?

Provide boxes of all shapes and sizes, wire netting, newspaper for papier mache, fur, materials for monsters. Make a gallery of wild things – large and small.

Look at teeth, claws and horns in books. Find some information on the internet about animals in the jungle with claws.

The circus comes to town

What you want the children to learn or develop
To move with coordination and control
To persevere in repeating some actions/attempts when developing a new skill

Linked areas of learning
Communication, Language and Literacy
Problem Solving, Reasoning and Numeracy

Themed links
Circus, Travelling, Performing, Journeys, Ourselves
Resources

Juggling balls
Windmill
Hoops
Bean bags
Ropes
Any equipment that promotes circus skills

This activity is best approached as part of a themed week/ fortnight. Prepare the children by explaining what a circus is. Best of all, take them to a real circus! Explain that the circus will be coming to their outdoor area! Advertise this a week before so that parents have the chance to become involved – supplying props, making costumes, and so on. The children can make advertising posters, tickets and signs.

Set up the role-play area outside with a tent, a ticket office, café/ ice cream van. Encourage plenty of free play with the equipment such as juggling balls, plate spinning, tightrope walking (a rope along the floor!), diablo.

Eventually set the children the challenge of putting on a circus show for everyone. Invite parents/carers and people from the local community.

This type of play is excellent for those children who need time to stand back and observe first before they try it at their own pace, without feeling under pressure. Some children will go back time and time again to practise a skill.

Allow the children to organise their own activities for the show, intervening when necessary but taking into account all of their ideas.
Involve all of the children who want to take part – don't forget the ringmaster!

Messages

What you want the children to learn or develop
To manipulate objects (a rope) by picking up, arranging and threading

Linked areas of learning
Communication, Language and Literacy
Problem Solving, Reasoning and Numeracy

Themed links
Shapes, Islands
Set the scene: some children are stranded on an island and they have decided to write a message to passing

Resources
Lengths of dowling about half a metre long
An area of soft earth or pots filled with sand for each piece of dowling to stand in
Re-usable adhesive
A long length of rope or a French skipping rope (elasticated) helicopters – to attract attention so that they can be rescued! (For more details, see pages 48-49.)

Help the children to set up a grid pattern with the dowling in the ground. Talk with them about being careful because the sticks could be dangerous - put lumps of adhesive on the top of each if necessary. Show them how to wind the rope around the grid so that letters/shapes can be formed.

Give them time to experiment with the ropes and see what shapes they can make.

- Young children will just enjoy putting the rope on and off and manipulating the ropes around the sticks.
- Extend the activity by asking them eventually if they can make the letter 'H' for 'Help' or SOS!
- What other suggestions do they come up with? Be prepared to listen.
- This activity is great fun and can be practised on small boards with elastic bands indoors or outside.

Scavenger hunt

What you want the children to learn or develop
To be able to fill a small bag and open and close it

Linked areas of learning
Problem Solving, Reasoning and Numeracy
Knowledge and Understanding of the World

Themed links
Counting, or any story or topic

Resources
As many small drawstring bags as can be found (the kind supplied for use with washing powder tablets)
A variety of objects - both natural and made - with corresponding picture cards
A game to play at any time

Most children love the idea of collecting things in small bags. These are excellent because they are strong and will stand a certain amount of rough and tumble.

Show the children how to open and close the bags. Make up a chart or have a group of objects out for the children to see what they are going to collect. It could be small stones, coloured plastic treasure nuggets or leaves. They could collect farm animals that have escaped from the farm, wild animals that have wandered away from the safari park! They could look for objects that are all the same colour. To develop number skills they could be asked to find three leaves, six fir cones, and so on.

Put cards in the bags showing what the children are to collect, for example a picture of a shell or a card showing a number.

Make it a challenge for some children by using a timer. They can hang their bags from a washing line or fence.

As the children become used to opening and closing the bags, talk to them about what other types of closing mechanisms are found on bags and make a collection, for example clasp bags, zip-up bags, and so on.

Parachute games

What you want the children to learn or develop
To develop coordination and self-confidence in relation to space

Linked areas of learning
Communication, Language and Literacy
Problem Solving, Reasoning and Numeracy

Themed links
Games/toys, Transport, Circles, Shapes, Fairground, Parks, Colour

Resources
A small parachute
A large beach ball

Parachute games are hugely enjoyed by children of all ages. The concept of parachute play may be introduced to very young children through circle games and activities that involve hoops and ropes (small groups may be created by tying a number of ropes to a hoop). Here are some simple activities to try with a small parachute:

Gently wave the parachute up and down.

Walk around in one direction with the parachute held at different levels.

Changing direction on a signal.

Named children run to the middle and back to their place. Named children change places by running under.

Give children a colour and ask colour groups to run into the centre or around the outside and back to their place.

Give children numbers/animal names/transport names and so on, and they run around the outside and back to their place.

Place a beach ball on the parachute and try to move it around the edge and back to the same place.

Roll a ball under the parachute to a named child.

Everyone sits on the floor and brings the parachute down to envelope everyone.

Make collections of leaves and put them on the top of the parachute – watch what happens when the parachute is moved up and down.

In all of these activities you will take the lead and encourage the children to listen and engage with them but there is considerable scope for them to be inventive and think of new games, too. They have to take turns and take account of what the others in the group are doing and it is quite physically demanding.

Aiming and throwing

What you want the children to learn or develop
To be able to aim and throw accurately

Linked areas of learning
Problem Solving, Reasoning and Numeracy
Communication, Language and Literacy

Themed links
This game can be linked to any topic.

Resources

A selection of containers, for example three different-sized boxes, baskets or bins
A variety of apparatus that can be thrown, such as small and large balls, bean bags, balls made from scrunched-up paper
Number cards/pictures
Starting place – rope, chalk line

Place different-sized containers a few metres away from a chalk line or rope. Each container has a number card or picture attached, for example the small box might be worth three points and the large box one point.

Make sure there is a variety of apparatus available – both small and large/heavy and light. Encourage the children to practise throwing. Model throwing for them, talking it through.

- Make a game of it by challenging them to better their scores by the end of the week.
- Extend the activity by placing the containers further away or making them smaller.
- Have the activity around for at least a week so that children can go back to it time and time again.
- Use pictures to represent numbers, for example an aeroplane means two, a car three, and so on.
- Promote good habits by encouraging the children always to put the balls back ready for someone else to play.

Threading

What you want the children to learn or develop
To be able to manipulate and manage to thread cardboard tubes through holes

Linked areas of learning
Creative Development
Problem Solving, Reasoning and Numeracy
Communication, Language and Literacy

Themed links
Buildings, Homes, Underground

Resources

An assortment of large cardboard boxes
A variety of long and short cardboard tubes (the inner tubes of lengths of materials, rolls of carpets or tubes that hold posters)

Cardboard box play is versatile and most children will spend many an hour messing around with boxes. Imaginations can take off and the really large boxes are so much fun – to be able to get inside with your friends is magical! They are light but fairly strong and can be turned upside down or placed on their side by the smallest of children. The boxes can be collected and stored flat until needed. Holes of various sizes need to be cut into the sides of the boxes at different levels beforehand. Take the boxes inside at the end of the session, but otherwise leave them outside all the time - they are easy to replace when worn out.

- Encourage the children to play with the equipment as they want.
- Model, if necessary, how the tubes can fit through the holes.
- Be prepared to help those children that find manoeuvering the tubes difficult and encourage them to talk about what they are doing.
- Take the opportunity to extend the children's vocabulary by hypothesising with them about whether the tubes will fit or not. Is this hole too narrow or wide enough for the tube? What do you think?

These types of construction play activities are brilliant for role play and children have enormous fun building fire engines, trains, and re-enacting all kinds of scenarios. If tarpaulins and blankets are added play can be extended to include tunnels and cave-like areas.

Streamers

What you want the children to learn or develop
To be able to demonstrate spatial awareness and have a sense of balance

Linked areas of learning
Creative Development
Knowledge and Understanding of the World

Themed links
Weather, Shapes, Sounds

Resources
Lengths of dowling, narrow broom handles or thin branches
Streamers made from ribbons, kite material, supermarket carrier bags or any such material cut into strips

Make the streamers by fixing the material to the lengths of dowling. The children can make their own – rolling the end of the material around the stick and just needing some help with the fastening. Cut dowling can be fairly sharp at the end so care will be needed. The ends can be sandpapered or filed to make them less sharp.

The streamers can be used in a variety of ways to encourage the children to stretch and use their muscles. They are fun just to play with and an adult modelling how to use them will greatly enhance the play.

The children will need space and should be encouraged to look around to be careful not to hurt anyone.

Later all kinds of activities can be encouraged:

- Make wiggly lines, straight lines, zigzags
- Make circles, high and low
- Draw letter shapes - let them guess yours
- Stretch up to the sky/across to the side
- Follow my leader
- Play mirror images with a partner
- Move to music

If children run around with the streamers they can watch them stream out behind them – especially good for a windy day and with longer lengths!

Encourage them to show each other the movements they can make. Can they spell their name? Can their friend guess what shape they are making?

Vehicles

What you want the children to learn or develop
To develop coordination skills and be able to steer around a course

Linked areas of learning
Problem Solving, Reasoning and Numeracy
Creative Development

Themed links
Journeys, Transport, Myself

Resources
Any type of wheeled toys - bikes, prams, trailers
Markers, bollards, ropes, planks, tyres
Chalks, masking tape

Set up a course for the children to travel around. Any type of equipment can be used but it needs to be stable and as realistic as possible. Masking tape is useful for marking lines/grids/road junctions on tarmac surfaces and can be easily removed. Make sure that the course is set up in a place where it will not interfere with the other play in the area. It can be frustrating if someone moves the roadway inadvertently!

Trails are really fun and successful if linked to role-play areas. The quality of play can be excellent and long-lasting when it is realistic. Encourage the children to use the course in a safe way and set up or encourage a scenario so that it is purposeful, for example delivering letters, collecting dustbins, going to the garage.

- Talk with the children about their journeys and include positional language, such as 'Who was behind you?'
- Encourage those who are less confident at riding a bike to take you on the journey and you can help when necessary!

- When the children have had some practice, encourage them to make their own courses or trails. Supply the apparatus and be nearby ready to intervene when necessary so that if they need a roundabout, for example, you can supply the tyre!

Cardboard box city

What you want the children to learn or develop
To construct with large materials

Linked areas of learning
Communication, Language and Literacy
Creative Development

Themed links
Houses and homes, Buildings, Materials, 'The Three Little Pigs', 'Goldilocks and the Three Bears'

Resources
An assortment of cardboard boxes
Some sheets of card
Tools for cutting

This activity is open-ended and free. The children can build and construct whatever they want. Often children will have just one or two boxes to play with. If they have eight, nine or ten boxes the dynamics of the play is different and cooperative play is much more evident.

- Be prepared to take part in the play.
- Help with the cutting if necessary – they may want to put a roof on or make a front door.
- Encourage the children to talk about what they are doing.
- They can make a whole street with numbers on the front doors and engage in meaningful play in their own context.
- They may want to use the boxes to build other things such as forms of transport. Support this play by intervening only to help them create this extra dimension.

Planks, crates and tyres

What you want the children to learn or develop
To show an understanding of how to transport equipment safely

Linked areas of learning
Creative Development
Problem Solving, Reasoning and Numeracy

Themed links
Buildings, Materials

Resources
About 20 planks of wood
20 plastic crates
Car tyres

This is an open-ended activity – the children can play freely using their imagination, playing cooperatively. This is exciting play and will often last for days rather than a session. Be prepared to let this happen if necessary.

Make sure the planks are smooth and as splinter free as possible. Talk to the children about using the planks safely – if they need to move them they must be careful about who is behind. Safety is of paramount importance.

The planks, crates and tyres are all large and hefty and will need to be manoeuvred by the children. To be able to do this properly they will need to talk to each other and cooperate.

Ask the children to talk about what they are making/doing.

Activities to support Creative Development

Make a miniature garden

What you want the children to learn or develop
To be able to work creatively on a small scale

Linked areas of learning
Physical Development
Knowledge and Understanding of the World

Themed links
Gardens, Growth, Parks, Nursery rhymes, Big and little (Opposites)

Resources
An assortment of trays – shallow
Earth
Garden trowels, forks, watering can
Access to a variety of materials, such as twigs, leaves, flowers, shells, ribbons
Gravel, small stones

It is important that the children have access to lots of found materials for this activity. The object is to make a garden in a shallow tray and perhaps put it on display for the rest of the children and adults (including parents) to see.

Take the children for a walk in a local garden, park, school grounds or nursery setting to look at what is usually found in a garden. Then allow the children plenty of time to develop their own miniature garden.

- Encourage them to think about what they could use to represent items but always be prepared to accept their ideas.
- Capable children will enjoy drawing a plan first and then trying it out.
- Nursery rhymes such as 'Mary, Mary quite contrary', can be used as a starting point or any story with a garden connection, for example The Hungry Caterpillar.

- Encourage all the children to talk about what they have made and why they made their choices.

Clay modelling

What you want the children to learn or develop
To explore an experience using a range of senses

Linked areas of learning
Communication, Language and Literacy
Physical Development
Personal, Social and Emotional Development

Themed links
Buildings, Materials, Change,
Resources
Large surface covered with plastic sheeting
Clay
Board
Clay tools
Aprons
Drying place
Natural materials, for example pebbles, comes, shells, feathers, leaves

Prepare an area where the children can experiment with the clay and not have to worry about making a mess. A wallpaper table or trestle with cut-down legs covered with a plastic cloth is good as children can work on either side.

Allow the children time to play with the clay. Provide some natural materials for the children to use with the clay if they want, for example pebbles, cones, shells, feathers, sticks, twigs and leaves.

Encourage them to talk about how the clay feels to them. Get them to close their eyes – Does it feel the same? Does clay smell? What happens when feathers are stuck into some clay?

Many young children will just want to explore the clay without making an object. Let them feel it, shape it, describe it and see what it can do. Other children will be keen to mould it into a shape or make a sculpture incorporating natural materials. This can be linked to a topic, such as a story, or they can be challenged to make an object practising a particular technique.

It is always fun for children to try to make an object, perhaps relating to the theme of the week, but be careful not to influence their imagination too much and only intervene when it is really necessary.

Texture rubbing

What you want the children to learn or develop
To look closely at similarities and differences

Linked areas of learning
Physical Development
Knowledge and Understanding of the World
Problem Solving, Reasoning and Numeracy

Themed links
Patterns, Senses
Resources
Shells, bark, stones, leaves
Magnifying glasses
Rough textures in the outside area
Optional number labels
Crayons, chalks
Sheets of paper in different thicknesses and with different textures

Provide the children with a variety of different types of paper. Show them how to place their chosen paper over their chosen texture and rub with the crayon/chalk.

Allow the children plenty of time to experiment with the technique. Once they have mastered it, you can introduce numbered labels to lead the children around a trail. The trail can be made exciting by giving the children challenging textures to collect – in challenging places, for example inside a den, or somewhere not so easy to find.

- Encourage the children to talk about where they are going next.
- Discuss whether they have found some rubbings that look the same and why they think that might be.
- Talk about which paper produces the clearest rubbing.

Smelly boxes

What you want the children to learn or develop
To investigate using their sense of smell

Linked areas of learning
Communication, Language and Literacy
Knowledge and Understanding of the World
Problem Solving, Reasoning and Numeracy

Themed links
Senses, Journeys, Number lines, Treasure hunt

Resources
Up to 20 small boxes or containers with numbers on lids

Ingredients for smelling, for example mint, lavender, vinegar, smelly cheese, soap, rose petals, rosemary

Children love treasure hunts. This is a variation on the treasure hunt idea. Talk to the children about the boxes and show them some.

Explain that they are part of a game and that the boxes have to stay in their places. All of the boxes must be marked in some way – with numbers, colours, shapes, letters or pictures.

Place the boxes around the outdoor area – don't make them too difficult to find. Allow the children time to smell as many boxes as they want and to talk about them.

- The younger children might differentiate between smells they like and smells they don't like: 'I like the star box and the heart box. I don't like the dotty box'.
- The older children might be able to tell an adult what they think is in them, for example 'I think it's soap in the blue box' or 'There's chocolate in number 3'.
- Challenge some children to find the box that has the curry powder!

Sounds

What you want the children to learn or develop
To recognise and explore how sounds can be changed

Linked areas of learning
Communication, Language and Literacy
Knowledge and Understanding of the World

Themed links
Weather, Sounds, Materials

Resources
Lengths of plastic drainpipe
Copper piping
Wood pieces
Chains
Pebbles
Dried leaves
Metal spoons
Any other materials

Make a collection of a wide variety of materials that will make interesting sounds. Allow the children time to just play and experiment with the items.

Provide a scenario for the children to work with, for example a story that has a windy day or a thunderstorm, and suggest that they make the appropriate sounds. What could they use?

Ask questions such as 'What sound will it make if you put that chain down the copper pipe?'

- Talk about soft sounds and loud sounds.
- Talk about sounds they like to make and ones they don't.
- Talk about how they can make sounds change.
- Encourage them to make repeated patterns.
- Stand back and allow them to make as much noise as they want!

Weaving

What you want the children to learn or develop
To investigate and use a variety of media

Linked areas of learning
Physical Development
Communication, Language and Literacy
Problem Solving, Reasoning and Numeracy

Themed links
Pattern, Materials

Resources
A frame made from branches and rope, chain link fence or wooden fence posts
Ribbons, ropes, long grasses, feathers, plastic carrier bags, leaves

Make a large weaving frame from branches tied together with string between, from lengths of dowling and string, or there may be some fencing that could be used. Explain to the children that they could weave materials between to make an attractive display. Show them how to do it.

Discuss what could be used to weave and be open to all suggestions. Go on a walk for them to collect long grasses and leaves.

Make a collection of ribbons, feathers, coloured strips of paper and materials, cut up carrier bags and have an ongoing supply of materials.

- Be available to help out when a child needs to be untangled!
- Have a wide variety of materials available.
- Allow the activity to carry on as long as the interest is still there – a day, a week or a month!
- Encourage the children to think about the patterns they are making.
- Encourage some of them to make their own small weaving frames and decorate with whatever they want. These can be hung from ceilings or porches outside as mobiles.
- Discuss why some things are easier to weave than others.

Painters and decorators

What you want the children to learn or develop
To be able to work collaboratively on a large and small scale

Linked areas of learning
Communication, Language and Literacy
Problem Solving, Reasoning and Numeracy
Knowledge and Understanding of the World

Themed links
Houses and homes, People who help us, Patterns, Seaside

Resources
Paintbrushes, large and small
Paint rollers
Empty, clean paint containers
Food colouring
Hard hats
Overalls
Clipboards, writing implements
Decorators' table
Goggles

Paint colour swatches
Colour brochures and booklets

Ask the children: 'I wonder what we could do to make this place look better?' There may be somewhere outside that they could brighten up themselves, such as an old wall, the inside or outside of a shed, a neglected corner. Talk about what they would like and why.

Encourage them to think about what they would need and where they could get the things from.

Encourage them to put forward their own views and plan so that all of the children's ideas are taken into account and recorded – on tape maybe?

- Make a list of their suggestions and refer to them as the project develops. Take photos before, during and after the project.
- Set up the area so that the children can access the materials of their choice.
- Be prepared to allow them to try out their own ideas.
- Be aware of what they need so that the learning experience can be as focused as possible.

Once they have finished, the children could repeat the project as a role-play scenario. Provide large boxes, sheets of cardboard, old chairs and tables for them to work on and decorate together. Old chairs bought from junk shops or car boot sales are wonderful for decorating and working on and can be used over and over again.

Making mobiles

What you want the children to learn or develop
To be imaginative and make choices about a range of materials

Linked areas of learning
Physical Development
Knowledge and Understanding of the World
Problem Solving, Reasoning and Numeracy

Themed links
Weather, Colour, Light

Resources
Any clear plastic containers, for example balls, bells, small boxes, laminating pouches, plastic bags
Collections of materials such as brightly coloured feathers, ribbons, threads, leaves, coloured stones and pebbles
Twigs and wool

The children choose a container and fill it with anything they like. Hang them from trees, fences or in windows. The balls make attractive mobiles. Spread the collection around the outdoor area so the children can look for their own items.

Encourage the children to think about the sizes of the things they are collecting.

They might want to find things that are the same colour or all natural.

- Make up your own collection alongside the children and model how you are deciding what to put in your container.
- If you have laminating pouches, set up the laminator or ironing board so that the children can see what happens when their pouch is heated
- Talk to them about what they think might happen when it is heated.
- Have them on display for all to see.

The balls are pretty when filled with coloured water and hung from trees so that the light shines through. The children can thread ribbons through the holes in the tops and choose where to hang them.

Pebble painting

What you want the children to learn or develop
To be able to work creatively on a small scale

Linked areas of learning

Physical Development
Communication, Language and Literacy

Themed links

Materials, Seaside, Rocks

Resources

An assortment of smooth pebbles
Chalks
Paint
Charcoal
Paintbrushes
Short twigs
Bowl of water

Before the children begin to paint or decorate their pebble they could first find it! Allow the children to choose one they like and to study it carefully. If it was taken away, would they recognise it again? Does it have any special marks? Pebbles have such a lovely smooth feel that children often just enjoy handling them, making patterns or lines and ordering them.

Encourage the children to handle the pebbles, feeling their weight and size. Encourage them to describe them.

If they would like to decorate the pebbles, give them a variety of materials to choose from. The pebbles can be painted with patterns, made to represent an animal, bird, insect, flower or anything at all. Numbers or letters painted on pebbles can be used for all kinds of games.

Some children may want to experiment with charcoal or chalk, others will enjoy washing their pebble in a bowl of water.

Shoe prints

What you want the children to learn or develop

To understand that different media can be combined

Linked areas of learning

Physical Development
Communication, Language and Literacy
Personal, Social and Emotional Development

Themed links

Stories such as 'The Elves and the Shoemaker', 'Jack and the Beanstalk', 'The Old Woman who Lived in a Shoe'; topics such as Shoes, Materials, Weather, Clothes

Resources

A selection and assortment of shoes
Paint
Shallow trays
Washing bowl and towel
Large sheets of paper

The children can have such fun mixing and matching pairs of shoes. They can make patterns and footprints by wearing the shoes, stepping in a tray of paint and then straight onto a sheet! Have plenty of water and towels available!

Make sure the children's clothes are protected. Model what the children could do. Talk about the patterns that are made, the similarities and differences.

- Count how many footprints they can make with one step in the paint.
- Can they make a wiggly line, a circle, a straight line?
- Which shoe would they choose for a giant?